P9-EAO-789

To

From

On the occasion of

VIP: How to Influence with Vision, Integrity, and Purpose

Published in Nashville, Tennessee, by Thomas Nelson. Thomas Nelson is a registered trademark of HarperCollins Christian Publishing, Inc.

Cover design by Koechel Peterson & Associates, Minneapolis, Minnesota.

Thomas Nelson titles may be purchased in bulk for educational, business, fund-raising, or sales promotional use. For information, please e-mail SpecialMarkets@ThomasNelson.com.

ISBN-13: 978-0-7180-7849-2

Printed in China

16 17 18 19 20 DSC 5 4 3 2 1

How to Influence with
Vision, Integrity, and Purpose

O. S. HAWKINS

DEDICATION

To Six Really GRANDkids

JACKSON, our first: His heart of compassion and love inspires me every day. If I had to describe what I want in a grandson, I would simply type out what he is!

HALLE: If there is a kid anywhere who loves to learn and explore more than she does, I haven't met her yet. Her bright mind encourages me to study more myself . . . just to keep up!

JULIA: This beautiful young lady has the gift of mercy and help like no other. She is always in tune with those around her and longing to help in any way.

HAYES: This tenderhearted young man will melt your heart with just his facial expressions. Sweetness.

AUDREY: Now here is a package of love and affection! She prides herself in being our tomboy and just may be one of the best athletes in the fold.

TRUETT: We thought we were finished and then this little dude came along. We are so glad he did. He is so full of life! He is going to keep us all younger for a little longer.

Susie and I are really proud to be their Honey and Poppy. We are praying that all of them become VIPs in their own right as they find the will of God for their lives . . . and do it!

CONTENTS

All royalties from this book are donated to Mission:Dignity, which supports pastors, their wives, and their widows in their declining years who are in financial need. Visit www.guidestone.org and click on Mission:Dignity for more information.

INTRODUCTION

Acronyms! We who speak the English language are obsessed with them. In fact, in every facet of life, we are hard-pressed to communicate without them. When we were in elementary school, our parents went to PTA. If we grew up in a rural area, we participated in FFA. When we hoped to get into the college of our choice to earn a BA, we paid careful attention to our GPA and studied hard for the SAT. Sportscasters would be at a loss for words without talking about a pitcher's ERA, a hitter's RBI, or a kicker's PAT. In business we speak of a man or woman who is a CEO, a COO, or a CFO who holds a CPA degree. In the political world, the president is POTUS and the Supreme Court is SCOTUS. We communicate with one another with FAQ, FYI, and IMO, and we conclude our letters with a PS. In the health arena, men should frequently check their PSA. Those in the military who desert their post are AWOL. We sit at the lunch counter and order a BLT. And what would church life have been the past several decades without VBS? Then, of course, the new social media craze has a language all its own . . . LOL.

Perhaps no other single acronym has muscled and maneuvered its way into our mainline English vernacular like VIP (very important person) has. Being important seems to be the personal goal of many who are climbing from rung to rung up the ladder of perceived success and recognition. This insatiable desire for importance is virtually universal. We have seen it in business circles; it is more than obvious in athletics; it is grossly revealed in politics. Even in ecclesiastical circles this desire for importance too often raises its ugly head. Yes, to have others see us as important is the driving force for many of us and, unfortunately, is the root of the destruction and demise of too many relationships.

This desire within each of us is nothing new. In fact, it predates mankind. One has to go back even before the beginning, way back into the eternal council of God in eternity past. Lucifer was an angel of light, "the seal of perfection, full of wisdom and perfect in beauty" (Ezekiel 28:12). He was placed by God Himself to be an important part, if not the leader, of the praise that was happening around the throne of heaven. But one day Lucifer decided he wanted to be a VIP. Motivated by pride and the desire to be somebody who was admired and exalted, he said, "I will be like the Most High" (Isaiah 14:14)—and Lucifer was expelled from heaven, thrust out forever. But gifted with the power of persuasion, he enticed one-third of all the angelic hosts to join him in his prideful rebellion (Revelation 12:4). Today we know this fallen angel as Satan, and when our first parents were walking in the garden of Eden, he appeared and successfully tempted them to follow suit. We inherited our sin nature from Adam and Eve, and that nature has its own subtle and sinister way of playing into our own pride.

We came by our prideful desire to be important honestly, and we learned it early. Taking our first steps as babies opened the door to the arena of center stage for each of us. And we liked it! We liked the applause, we liked the affirmations, and we liked the adoration. So we took another step . . . then another. Being the center of attention—being the most important one in the room—had and continues to have quite an appeal.

This unquenchable thirst for importance doesn't end when we learn to walk. It stays with us for a lifetime. It shows up in all sorts of self-promoting ways no matter how subtle we may be. As we grow older, this VIP syndrome, as I call it, pushes us to want the perceived comforts of being separate from the more common types; it drives us to want the best seats in the house; it fuels our sense of being entitled. We can be absolutely consumed by the desire to be noticed and recognized—to be a very important person.

If, by chance, you are reading these words and thinking they are directed toward someone else, let me ask you a few questions. How often do you check your Facebook, Twitter, or other social media pages? After you post something, do you hurry back to see how many "likes" you have, how many "favorites" are listed, or how many pats on the back you received? Does the number of "likes" have any impact on how you feel about yourself during the day? If we were truly honest, most of us would have to admit to at least a little bit of ego-driven narcissism, and social media can help us recognize that in ourselves. Today's social media craze has a dual effect on our culture. Facebook, for example, can be a great tool for reestablishing relationships that have lain dormant for years. But in too many cases, this desire within us for importance has led to the destruction of longtime relationships, even marriages. More than one divorce has occurred due to someone reconnecting with an old high school sweetheart after many years.

For any of us who may be thinking we are already pretty important, let me say that everything is relative. Case in point, standing on the beach in South Florida and gazing at the Atlantic Ocean, we are overwhelmed by its massive power and its vastness stretching before us, thousands and thousands of miles, to the horizon and beyond. But is the Atlantic really that large? The next time we lull ourselves to sleep with our own false sense of self-worth and self-importance, let's remember this: We might think the Atlantic is big; our earth, huge; and our planetary system, vast; but the known universe is home to at least ten trillion other systems like ours. In reality, then, the earth is a very tiny planet. (In fact, there are planets in our own solar system that one thousand earths could fit inside!) Furthermore, our own solar system, with its eight planets revolving around our sun, is only a very small dot in a very tiny corner of the Milky Way galaxy. The Milky Way is over 120,000 light-years wide and contains at least 100 billion planets, and it is but a *speck* in a super cluster of galaxies we call the observable universe. And—to stretch your mind a bit further—what we know and can observe of this vastness is nothing in relationship to infinity!

And in the midst of all this are some strange little creatures standing on their hind legs, consumed with their self-importance, wanting to be noticed, and desiring to be VIPs. The next time you're feeling pretty important, go to your computer and Google "Messenger Spacecraft 2005 video" and watch this YouTube video of the earth receding into the cold, black darkness of space until it is out of sight. Not even a trace. Still interested in becoming a VIP? In light of all that is around us, our own importance is a bit relative, to say the least.

One of the greatest stories ever told is commonly referred to as the parable of the prodigal son. It was told by Jesus Christ and recorded for all posterity in Luke 15:11–32. There was a man who had two sons. The younger one became a bit bored at home. No doubt he had heard tales of the bright lights of the big cities. He took his inheritance and left home. What started out as a fun adventure ended—as it does so often—with all the money gone and nowhere to turn. The son's newfound homelessness and hunger caused him to beat the streets looking for work; he was desperate for anything that would put a few dollars in his pocket. Finally, he found a job—a not-too-pleasant one for a nice Jewish boy, but at least it was a job. He worked in a pigpen feeding the swine, and his hunger got so bad that he even started craving the rotten ears of corn the pigs were eating. That's when "he came to himself" and decided to head home, ask his dad for forgiveness, and apply for a job as one of the hired hands in the family business. Before he even reached the house, though, his father saw him walking up the road, ran off the porch toward him, forgave him instantly, hugged and kissed him, and threw a huge party in his honor, saying, "My son was lost, and now he is found!"

And it's too bad the story doesn't end there. Another character now takes center stage—the older brother. This young man had done everything right. He was obedient. He had stayed home and been faithful to the family. Yet he suffered from the VIP syndrome. I have noticed something about people who are on a quest for importance. They are a bit territorial about that spotlight, and they find it hard to rejoice when someone else is getting the attention. The older brother was angry and would not go to the party. Noticing this, the father went out, found him, and pleaded with him to join in the celebration. This older brother wanted the attention his brother was getting; he wanted to be appreciated and applauded. And we'll get back to him in a minute.

It matters not who you are or where you are from, we all have three very important kinds of relationships in life. The first has an *outward* dimension. These are the relationships we have with other people at home, in the office, in the social arena. We are made to connect with one another—to be in close and dynamic interpersonal relationships. The second is the *inward* dimension, and this is the relationship we have with ourselves. Some call it self-respect, or self-worth, or even self-importance. (The truth is that much of what goes wrong in our outward expression of relationships is because of what is going on inside us at a given time!) Finally, there is the *upward* dimension. We have the capacity to enter into a relationship with God Himself through Jesus Christ and then know Him with the intimacy of a Father and His child. This amazing reality is what separates us from all the rest of the created order. Tragically, becoming consumed with one's self-importance can have a devastating effect on every relationship in life, in every dimension. Now back to the older brother . . .

The quest to become a VIP can *destroy* our relationships with others because it destroys our own joy and happiness. Look at this older brother. He was "angry" (Luke 15:28), and gone was his smile. But that is not all. The whole place was exploding with joy and excitement, but he "would not go in" (v. 28). Not only does the desire to be important destroy our happiness, but it often destroys our helpfulness as well. He didn't lift a finger to help with, not to mention enjoy, the celebration. And clearly the older brother's behavior destroyed the harmony of the home. When we live in a small world bordered on the north and south, east and west, with self-importance, it has a destructive effect on our relationships with people.

As for our relationship with ourselves, our quest to become a VIP can *distort*. First, wanting to be important distorts our vision. Consider again the older brother's words and how they were laced with the perpendicular pronoun *I*. Listen to him: "These many years *I* have been serving you; *I* never transgressed your commandment . . . you never gave *me* a young goat, that *I* might make merry with *my* friends" (v. 29, emphasis mine). I . . . I . . . me . . . I . . . my! Feeling like we are important keeps us from seeing past ourselves. But not only does the quest for importance distort our vision, but it also distorts our virtue. This older brother was thinking only in terms of what he thought he deserved—a definite sign of someone with a VIP complex. It is always a dangerous thing to move off the foundation of grace and into the arena of what we think we deserve.

Finally, the quest to become a VIP can *deceive* us about our relationship with God. We can come to feel so important and so capable that we wrongly think that somehow we can do life all on our own and we do not need to depend on Him. Yet hear how the father in our story gave his older son three promises to keep everything in perspective—and these are the same three promises our heavenly Father gives us. First, "Son, you are always with me" (v. 31). The Father promises His presence with us, always abiding. What a promise. But there is more: "And all that I have is yours" (v. 31). We have God's abundant provision. And then the father reminds his son of his brother's ultimate and now fulfilled purpose: "Your brother was dead and is alive again, and was lost and is found" (v. 32). When we become obsessed with our own importance, we become deceived into thinking we do not need God or His provision for us, nor do we have much to do with His purpose. It becomes mostly just about me.

And so the story ends. Rather abruptly too. Suddenly it's over, and we are left hanging. We don't know whether the older son went into the party and embraced his brother or whether he stayed away. Perhaps the story ends like this so each of us can complete the story for ourselves.

And thus we come to the heart of this volume: I want to redefine the acronym VIP in another, much more impactful manner. In the first place, my own premise is that *VIP* never should have been defined as a Very Important Person. I am convinced that VIP should be redefined as a *Very Influential Person*. The pursuit of importance often reveals a deep-seated inner need to be accepted and recognized. Working toward being important in the eyes of others is a self-absorbing and never-ending task. The need for just a little more applause, just another pat on the back, is never satisfied. Becoming a person of influence—a very influential person—will enable us to leave a richer, more lasting legacy. As far as I can tell, the world soon forgets those who are merely important. But it has a long memory when it comes to people who are truly influential.

Etymologically, our English word *influence* comes from a compound of two Latin words that are translated "in" and "flow." This brings to mind a word picture of a mighty and vibrant, crystal-clear river that runs deep and wide. Its rapid current flows powerfully, circumventing any and all obstacles in its way. This river is fed by numerous smaller creeks and streams that arrive at the river and virtually empty themselves into it, letting themselves be caught up in its flow. Influence works like that: you live your life in such a vibrant manner that those who come into contact with you become caught up in your flow.

In writing to the ancient Corinthians, and to us, the apostle Paul pointed to the fact that each of us has been assigned a specific sphere of influence. Paul taught that we should "boast only with regard to the area of influence God assigned to us" and prayed that "our area of influence among you may be greatly enlarged" (2 Corinthians 10:13, 15 ESV). Put this book down in your lap and think about that for a moment: God has assigned a specific area of influence to *you*! This is not some nebulous, esoteric kind of undefined influence. This is a specific area of influence where no one can be as effective as you. There is someone you can influence like no one else in this world can. No matter who you are, where you live, who you know, or what you do, the God of the universe has assigned a sphere of influence just to you. It may well be you have never thought of this, but recognizing and living out this truth can be life changing both for you and the people you influence. So what will you do about the fact that God has assigned to you an area where He desires that someone somewhere gets caught up in your flow?

The journey to becoming a true VIP is now before us. You *can* become a Very Influential Person, someone known for V-Vision, I-Integrity, and P-Purpose. Let's begin the journey. Others are waiting to get caught up in your flow.

There is someone
you can influence like no
one else in this world can. No
matter who you are, where you
live, who you know, or what you
do, the God of the universe has
assigned a sphere of influence
just to you.

V=Vision

Those who create a winsome and lasting influence on the people around them are men and women of vision. They know where they are going. And, even more important, they know how they plan to get there. As I stated in the introduction, people of influence are like a vibrant river in whose flow others are not simply caught up, but they are carried away. In turn, it is difficult to persuade anyone to let themselves get caught up in your flow if you have little idea of where you are headed, much less how you plan to arrive at your intended destination. Vision is vital when it comes to being a person of influence. "Where are we headed?" is a valid question, and people with influence have a common characteristic: they have a definitive answer to that question.

Ancient Israel's King Solomon—purported to be the wisest man who ever lived—understood the value of vision. One of the proverbs this man of influence left us almost three thousand years ago says this: "Where there is no vision, the people perish" (Proverbs 29:18 KJV). The word translated from Hebrew into English as *vision* appears thirty-five times in the Hebrew Bible, which Christians refer to as the Old Testament. The word carries the idea of a perception—a vision—not of what we are right now but of what we could become. According to *Strong's Hebrew Lexicon*, the word's root meaning is "to mentally perceive; to contemplate." Those with vision are men and women who do not see situations and circumstances only as they are now, but as they could be.

Solomon continued: where there is no spirit of conquest, where there is no vision, the people "perish." The Hebrew word for *perish* is more often translated "to go back." It is used, for instance, in Numbers 14:3 (ESV) to describe the group of Israelites in the wilderness who wanted to "go back" to Egyptian bondage even after experiencing the miracle of crossing the Red Sea on dry land. Solomon is reminding us across the centuries that people who have no mental perception of what they could become or what they could accomplish tend to meander through life with no forward direction or perceived purpose. They merely exist from day to day with little or no sense that anything significant lies ahead. These individuals who live without a vision have little perception of what they could become and no real direction in life. They influence few, if any, people around them. People of influence, however, cast a vision of what God wants them to be, where He wants them to go in life, and how He wants them to get there—and others get caught up in their flow.

Perhaps there are few figures in modern American history who had more fervent and loyal followers and, at the same time, more fearful and livid foes than my friend Jerry Falwell of Lynchburg, Virginia. A man of vision, he rose to public prominence in the 1980s when his Moral Majority—and the religious right that found its voice as a result—contributed significantly to the election of Ronald Reagan as president. In 1971 he had started a small Bible college at his local church in Lynchburg. While many thought him foolish and unrealistic, Falwell had a clear and grand vision for that struggling little school. He traversed the country sharing his vision. He spoke of a school that would one day be to evangelical believers what Brigham Young is to Mormons and what Notre Dame is to our Catholic friends. A few bought into his vision early on, but most thought it only hype, just hopeful rhetoric. Then dozens, then scores, then hundreds, then thousands of people started sending their students and their dollars in support of what today is Liberty University: they became caught up in his flow.

Recently I was invited to speak at the spring baccalaureate and commencement services at what is now called Liberty University. I had not been on the campus since Dr. Falwell's death and the accompanying funeral service in 2007. As the new president, Jerry Falwell Jr., a brilliant lawyer and educator with degrees from the University of Virginia, walked my wife and me across the campus, I could not believe my eyes. Today Liberty University is spread over thousands of beautiful acres. It has become the largest Christian university in the world with more than one hundred thousand students from every field of study imaginable. Even at this writing, hundreds of millions of dollars of new construction is in process—and Liberty remains debt free. Beautiful dormitories reach to skyscraper heights. The campus is filled with up-to-date athletic facilities, including a football stadium, a thirteen-thousand-seat basketball arena, an ice hockey arena, one of the finest baseball stadiums in America, and on and on I could go. The new medical school sits on Liberty Mountain, and down in the valley is the law school. Liberty's graduates are scattered far and wide, impacting lives for the good in every field of endeavor.

As we walked across the campus that day, I thought much of my friend. My first inclination was to exclaim, "How I wish Falwell could see Liberty University today! But before I said the words, I thought, *He* did *see it—and that's why it's*

Those with
vision are men and women
who do not see situations
and circumstances only as
they are now, but as
they could be.

all here! Vision is the *V* in becoming a VIP, a very influential person.

Before every great undertaking, someone—a VIP—has a vision for the task ahead. Think about it. The winning football coach has a game plan before kickoff—a vision of what he wants his team to accomplish and how to do it. The military commander envisions the strategy before the battle ever begins. The artist has an idea in his or her mind before the brush ever touches the canvas. But many individuals simply exist: they go to work, attend meetings, follow schedules, and something is missing. So often we simply cannot put our finger on it. What is it? I think it is vision. Having a vision for one's life is vital to living a worthwhile life, and those who influence others in life have a vision. They are able to see the end from the beginning, and they reach the end with a spirit of conquest.

History is replete with accounts of how one man or one woman inspired entire nations. Consider Sir Winston Churchill. When in London years ago, I visited his underground war rooms. Still on his old desk from those dark days of World War II is the little placard with words that reminded him daily of his vision for victory, the words of Queen Victoria's prime minister during the Boer War: "There is no depression in this house and we are not interested in the possibilities of defeat—they do not exist!" And who can forget his famous speech when he said,

"Never give in—never, never, never, never, in nothing great or small, large or petty, never give in except to convictions of honour and good sense." Visionaries like Israel's Golda Meir, our own Ronald Reagan, Russia's Mikhail Gorbachev, Britain's Margaret Thatcher, influenced entire nations and lifted them to new heights by holding forth a powerful and positive vision that led them to believe again in themselves and their future.

The Bible itself offers story after story of the impact of visionary leaders on others.

- Joshua and Caleb were two of the twelve Moses sent to spy out the land of Canaan upon their exodus from Egypt. Their ten friends returned and reported to Moses what *was:* walled, impenetrable cities and warriors who appeared to be giants, along with other related impossibilities. But Joshua and Caleb saw not simply what was, but also what could be and would be if they simply followed their God-given vision.

- Abraham influenced and is therefore revered by the three great world religions: Judaism, Christianity, and Islam. He played a key role in Old Testament history because he was a man of vision. God promised Abraham that he would become the father of a great nation of people (Genesis 12:1–3). But there was a problem—and it wasn't insignificant. Abraham was already an old man and his wife was barren: they weren't able to conceive a child. But God instructed Abraham to look up at the stars in the night sky and hold to the vision that his seed would become just as numerous (Genesis 15:5). Abraham did . . . and *it* did! He never let go of his vision; he believed God's promises.

- Joseph influenced two of the world's most progressive nations because he held to his vision for leadership. When Joseph was seventeen, God gave him a dream that showed he would be the leader of a great nation, and he never let go of it . . . even in the dark days when it seemed an utter impossibility.

- And there's Simon Peter, a fisherman who had a vision for the church. The first time our Lord saw his rough ways and callused hands, Jesus referred to him as a small pebble. Jesus also foresaw that Simon would

> become a great rock, so He gave him a new name: Peter. The same Lord looks at you even now—as you read these words—in the same way He looked at Simon Peter. Jesus does not only see you for who and what you are today, but He sees who you could become and what you can accomplish.

No one has ever walked the face of this earth who has influenced more people across the centuries than Jesus Christ. He left us with a huge vision and an accompanying large task. He challenged a small group of ragtag followers, who were basically an uneducated group, to reach an entire world with the good news of His gospel. Talk about a visionary! Their commission—and ours also, by the way—was not simply to go after a few locals, but entire nations all over the globe. This vision is even more amazing when we consider the challenge was given to men like James and John, Peter and Andrew. They were just local fishermen from the countryside and were joined by men like Matthew from the local IRS office. They adopted Christ's vision and ran with it all the way across the Roman Empire in a single generation. Without such modern conveniences as air travel, television, the Internet, and cell phones, they changed their world in their own lifetime. And when they all died, those they influenced kept telling the story and somebody told

Jesus challenged a small group of ragtag followers, who were basically an uneducated group, to reach an entire world with the good news of His gospel. Talk about a visionary!

someone else this good news . . . and someone told someone else . . . and someone told someone else… and someone told someone else. And that telling has continued for more than twenty centuries until it arrived at our own heart's door!

Those who have lasting influence on others are men and women of vision.

Most of us have, in one way or another, at one time or another, been challenged to "get a vision." Perhaps you heard it at a high-powered motivational meeting or sales seminar. But few of these events actually explain how to implement a vision, and a vision without an action plan is just a dream. Most of us have been there. We heard someone or read something, and got pumped up about what we could accomplish, but then had no real sense of how to make it happen. So this dream passed away like a hundred others before it. The converse is equally true: a task without a vision is pure drudgery. We all know people around us who know what they have to do, and they do it without a vision or any spirit of conquest. Consequently, the work—and maybe life itself—becomes simply mandatory and monotonous.

Since having a vision is vital to becoming a very influential person, how do we capture the concept? It is not that hard, really; let me explain. My wife, Susie, and I had the joy of seeing the birth of our two daughters. Thinking about the birth experience, I am convinced that their birth, as well as their growth, reflects the evolution of a vision. If you desire to become a person of vision, I believe you must understand that the first step in the birth of a vision is the same as the first step in the birth of a baby. A child's life as well as the onset of a vision begin at the moment of conception. The seed of a vision takes root in the mind and heart. For me this can be intentional and can happen when I consolidate all my facts, meditate on them, and seek to dream big dreams of what could be. Some of my own greatest dreams and visions, however, have come to mind in the natural flow of my own quiet devotional times and prayer life. God plants the seed of a vision in our hearts: conception takes place.

Nehemiah described that kind of experience. He had a civil service job and was comfortable with his benefits and retirement plans, but then he heard about Jerusalem's broken walls and burned gates. At that moment, his vision was conceived. He said, "I set out during the night with a few others. I had not told anyone what my God had put in my heart to do for Jerusalem" (Nehemiah 2:12 NIV). Just as God put Nehemiah's vision in his mind, God Himself will plant a vision, a desire, within our hearts. After all, He promised to "make known to

[you] the path of life" (Psalm 16:11 ESV). Having a vision means to see things not for what they are but for what they could be and will be! It is impossible to influence others without being a person of vision.

Whether we're talking babies or visions, gestation follows conception. During this extended time, the vision simply grows within us although others cannot see it for months. Nehemiah said he "told no one" (Nehemiah 2:12). Similarly, when Susie was pregnant with our daughter, we did not tell anyone for several months. In those first few months she was not showing, but our daughter Wendy was growing inside her. A man or a woman to whom God gives a vision needs a gestation period. During this time, we live with the vision. We allow it to grow inside us. We think on it. We meditate on it. We pray about it. We mull it over and over until it becomes more defined and solidified.

As I mentioned earlier, Joseph's life is a good example of someone in this gestation period. When Joseph was seventeen, God gave him the vision of what he would become. This idea grew in his heart for a long time, even when he lingered in an Egyptian dungeon and the possibility of its fulfillment seemed so far away. But Joseph never lost sight of it. We would be wise to follow his example. Once the vision is conceived in our mind and heart, we allow it to grow and develop, to fuel our passion and take more specific shape. After a while the people around us begin to see that something is happening, something is growing in us. Just as a mother-to-be can't rush the forty weeks of pregnancy, we who are parenting a vision can't rush its gestation. It is vital to the birth of both a baby and a vision.

Next comes the third stage in the life of a baby and a vision: birth! When the baby is actually born, we celebrate, hand out cigars, and send out the birth announcements. We don't give birth and keep quiet about it. Wanting everyone to know, we announce far and wide: "It's a boy!" or "It's a girl!" Likewise, after conception and gestation of our vision comes its birth, the moment when we present our personal vision for everyone to see. We carried it to term in our heart, and now we want people to know where we are leading them and how we are going to get there.

And what happens after the birth? Sometimes the answer to that question is a single word, one of the most beautiful words in our English language: *adoption*. This remarkable event is when individuals who have not been involved in the conception, the gestation, or the birth take the baby into their hearts and homes as though she were their own—and, by all legal rights, she is! The baby now takes their name because she is a part of their family. She is more theirs than anyone else's because they have adopted her. What a beautiful thing—and how very fortunate are those who know this experience!

What happens after the birth of a vision? Again, that question can be answered with that same beautiful word: *adoption.* This remarkable event is when individuals—who have not been involved in the conception, the gestation, or the birth—take the vision into their hearts. A vision is confined to an orphanage of ideas until it is adopted by others who are caught up in the flow of the one who birthed the vision.

Earlier in this chapter I introduced you to Jerry Falwell and the miracle on the mountain that is called Liberty University. I shall never forget the first time I met this dynamic man. It was the late 1970s, and I was the new, young, thirty-year-old pastor of the First Baptist Church in Fort Lauderdale, Florida. In those days the school was only seven or eight years old and still meeting in the facilities of the church Falwell pastored. He was serpentining the country telling the story of his vision to anyone and everyone who would listen. He had come to South Florida to host a luncheon meeting with local pastors. Rather reluctantly, and at the insistence of a pastor friend, I went to get a free lunch. I will never forget Falwell's passion and persuasiveness as he stood before us and painted a word picture not of what was but of what was going to be. I remember so well having

$2,200 in the bank, and it was all the cash Susie and I had to our name. After finishing his luncheon address, Dr. Falwell shared that for $2,000, you could become a member of the Founder's Club at Liberty. I had never before heard of the school, but then and there I adopted Jerry Falwell's vision of what Liberty was going to become. On the spot I wrote out a check for $2,000 and placed it in his hand. (It would take another complete volume to tell the story of how I tried to explain to my wife that evening that we were down to $200 because I had just gotten caught up in Jerry Falwell's flow!) Liberty exists today in large part due to his tireless efforts and the multiplied thousands who adopted his vision and came alongside him. People of influence are people of vision, and these people see their visions come to fruition when they are personally conceived, properly gestated, birthed, and then adopted by others.

Next comes the stage of growth. Once others adopt your vision as their own, a new synergy begins to happen. Your vision, like a baby, begins to grow. Anyone who has raised children knows that growth takes an awful lot of time, encouragement, energy, effort, and money! They outgrow clothes and shoes; their busy, full schedules keep us constantly on the move; and their growth means continual changes in our own lifestyles. So don't be surprised that the growth and development of your vision costs you time, energy, effort, and yes, money. Also, just as with the growth of a child, visions will experience some setbacks as they grow. Accidents happen when we are learning to walk, and we make mistakes in our adolescent years that we need to correct. But, by and large, the child and the vision continue to grow and grow.

Then, at some point, your vision reaches maturity. All you have dreamed about, hoped for, and prayed for comes to fruition. This stage of maturity is significant and rich, and I can point to a specific moment when I recognized that one of my visions had reached maturity. That moment was when I walked my daughter, in her beautiful white wedding gown, down the center aisle of the church and placed her hand into the hand of the young man who had won her heart. At that moment, the conception, the gestation, the birth, the growth, and all that went into raising that young woman came to maturity. When it comes to a vision, the stage of maturity is also significant and rich and very critical. Many people who have seen their dreams and visions come to maturity make a big mistake: they stop dreaming.

This brings us to the final step in the life cycle of children and visions, and that is reproduction. Susie and I have had the joy of seeing this stage happen in our own family. Our daughters have dreamed again for us by giving birth to our six grandchildren. And maybe you have had the joy of being the offspring of a visionary person: you were caught up in that person's flow, and then, in an act of reproduction, you shared that vision with others. Sometimes that happens; sometimes it doesn't. At this point a vision can cease to exist because it reached maturity and stopped growing, or that vision is reproduced into other visions—larger and grander visions—for the future.

Now you can see more clearly why influencers are men and women of vision. They know where they are going, and they have a plan for getting to their destination. Their vision began as yours will: listen to God in your heart and be sensitive to His leading as the seed of a vision is being planted in you. That vision will grow during a period of gestation when you meditate, think, and pray over it alone for a period of time. Next the vision is birthed and shared with others. Then hopefully your vision is adopted by those whom you influence. Your vision grows to maturity and, ideally, reaches a point when it is time to reproduce the process afresh and start all over again.

It's a story from history that we've heard since kindergarten, if not before . . .

Around four hundred years ago, a group of Pilgrims landed on the shores of America. Inspired by a tremendous God-given vision for freedom of worship and with great courage, they sailed uncharted seas in rickety wooden boats following their vision.

The seed of that vision had originally been given to William Bradford, the Pilgrim leader. During its gestational period, Bradford took time to think, meditate, consult Scripture, pray, dream, and plan. Then Bradford shared his vision with his congregation in the Netherlands. They celebrated this birth and wholeheartedly adopted the vision as if it were their own vision. The vision grew, and plans solidified. The Pilgrims boarded their boats and sailed into the unknown. The vision reached a point of maturity as they established their new colony on the eastern seaboard of the New World.

In their first year, the Pilgrims established a town and, in the second, a town council. In the third year the newly elected city government proposed the building of a road that would extend five miles west into the wilderness. The following year the citizens tried to impeach the council because they felt the expenditure of those road funds would be a waste of the public treasury. Somehow, in this relatively short time period, those forward-looking Pilgrims had lost their vision. Not long before, the Pilgrims had had a big enough vision to see across an entire ocean, but now they could not see even five miles into the wilderness. The Pilgrims had settled in and failed to reproduce;

Like the Pilgrims,
we can experience the
death of too many of our own
visions when they mature. The
cause of such death is our getting
comfortable and ceasing to
dream new dreams . . .

their initial vision was not followed up with grander, more far-reaching ones. Like the Pilgrims, we can experience the death of too many of our own visions when they mature. The cause of such death is our getting comfortable and ceasing to dream new dreams . . .

Be aware! The Pilgrims' experience wasn't all that unique. When we are growing a vision, we experience pressure at every stage along the way—pressure to abandon and abort, to retreat into the comforts and confinements of our familiar surroundings. Many visions don't come to life because the gestation was interrupted or cut short. Gestation takes time; it cannot be rushed. It also involves seeking the counsel of a few wise and trusted confidants. Very Influential People realize that each and every stage of birthing and growing their vision is vital to its having a long and productive life.

Vision is vital to the success of almost every endeavor. A lack of vision is what keeps many from becoming people of influence. As mentioned earlier, Solomon said it best: "Where there is no vision"—no concept of what God desires and intends us to be and do—"the people perish." Lacking any sense of forward direction, they go backward. Vision is vital to undertaking the task God has given you, and having that vision will do four distinct things for you.

Vision brings *definition*. When we truly capture the vision of what we can become and what we can accomplish, that vision defines our task; it clarifies what we are about. Many people formulate a one-sentence "vision statement" for their lives. This becomes the very lens that brings their lives into focus; it is the lens through which they view their choices and make their decisions.

At this writing I am in my eighteenth year of serving GuideStone Financial Resources as president and CEO. We serve those who serve the Lord all over the world by helping them with their financial and benefits service needs. Our more than 250,000 participants are pastors, church workers, missionaries, children's home workers, university and seminary professors, doctors, nurses, health care workers, and relief workers around the globe. We have formulated a simple vision statement that defines what we do: "GuideStone exists to honor the Lord by being a lifelong partner with our participants in enhancing their financial security." In this one sentence we find three important factors. First, we find our *motivation*: "We exist to honor the Lord." If every GuideStone worker honors the Lord, we will be well on our way to serving our clients with integrity and excellence. We also find our *message* in our vision statement: we desire to be a "lifelong partner with our participants." Those we serve give themselves to Christian care and causes, yet a large segment of them know very little about personal financial matters. That's why many of them think of us only as someone they will need someday long in the future when they reach vocational retirement. We are trying to change the way they think of us by teaching them about compound interest and encouraging them to get connected with us—and stay connected with us—throughout the various seasons of their lives. Finally, our vision statement points to our *mandate*: we are to "enhance their financial security." We are trying to get participants to a place of vocational retirement with enough financial security and dignity that they will not have to be on someone's relief roll. Our vision clearly defines our task and serves as the lens through which we decide what direction our company should go. In fact, when a new initiative is presented, we always ask three questions based on our vision statement: Will it honor the Lord? Will it help create the life partner concept? Will it ultimately enhance our participants' financial security? If not, we would not choose that course. Vision is vital: it will bring *definition* to your life.

Vision brings a new *dynamic*. Not much really happens without a vision. Life simply goes on rather uneventfully. It has been said, however, that life is like music. Some people live with a steady rhythm. They simply live day to day according to the same old monotonous beat. No real vision, no real dynamic, no spirit of conquest empowers them. As they continue with the same old same old, days stretch into weeks, weeks into months, and months into years. Other people, however, are like harmony. They go along with whatever is happening. They choose to blend in with the crowd, never making any noise that is not totally consistent with the whole. Finally, there are visionaries who give us a melody for life. They live with optimism, energy, and expectancy. They bring vibrancy to the score of life. Their vision gives them a compelling dynamic that energizes us every new and passing day.

A vision will also bring *direction* to our lives and tasks. "Where are you headed?" is a valid question. When our lives are guided by a personal, God-given vision, we can answer that question confidently because that vision brings with it a definite sense of purpose and direction. We know where we are headed, we have thought about how we plan to get there, and we have a purpose to guide us when we come to the intersections of life. People are prone to follow and let themselves be influenced by those who have a vision that brings definition to their lives, who live with a contagious energy, and who know where they are going. This direction that brings focus is a vital component of influence.

This element of focus is evident in the apostle Paul's New Testament letters to the believers of Colossae and Philippi. To the Colossians he said, "Set your mind on things above, not on things on the earth" (Colossians 3:2). In other words, Paul told them to focus not on the smaller, more trivial things that constantly swirl around them, but on the lasting things that bring life meaning and true purpose. To the Philippians he framed it thus: "I do not count myself to have apprehended; but one thing I do, forgetting those things which are behind and reaching forward to those things which are ahead, I press toward the goal for the prize of the upward call of God in Christ Jesus" (Philippians 3:13–14). He stayed focused on "one thing." Not five. Not three. Not even two. He referred to this "one thing I do." Interestingly, as he penned these words in Greek, he chose a very descriptive word that we translate as his "goal" in Philippians 3:14. We get our word *scope* from this Greek word. Like the scope on a rifle that focuses the shooter on the target, the great apostle was focused in his service to the Lord. Paul kept his vision square in the middle of the crosshairs of his scope.

My first pastorate was out on the plains of Southwestern Oklahoma at Hobart where the Comanche and Kiowa Indians once roamed and raided. Down on the town square was the A&B Coffee Shop where we often ate breakfast and lunch. In fact, once upon a time, every little village and every neighborhood in every city had such a coffee shop serving breakfast in the morning and sandwiches during the day. Three college buddies had a different idea for a coffee shop and opened their first Starbucks in Seattle in 1971. Ten years later Howard Schultz brought his professional experience and his vision of a different kind of coffee shop to the organization. In his crosshairs was his vision of a chain of coffee shops that focused on, of all things, coffee! And many of you reading these words right now will step into a Starbucks before the week, if not the day, is over.

All of us have probably had our frustrations with the slow delivery of the postal services. But a man in Memphis had a vision that focused on overnight delivery. Federal Express was born, and many of us will send or receive a FedEx package this week. This option exists because one man's vision brought direction and focus. Talk about influence! Influencers are men and women with a vision that defines their task, brings a new dynamic to their lives, and gives direction and focus to who they are and what they do.

A vision will not only bring definition, dynamic, and direction to your task, but it will also bring *dependence*. Your vision should be so God-sized that it drives you to a new dependence upon Him. In my own life, I have sought to have visions that were so big that there was little possibility of success without the Almighty's guidance and grace. A vision should stretch us beyond our own perceived ability to achieve so that, in the final analysis, we have to stand back and give God the glory for any and all of our accomplishments in life. In that final analysis, we would join the psalmist in exclaiming, "This was the LORD's doing; it is marvelous in our eyes" (Psalm 118:23).

So, you are interested in becoming a VIP . . . a Very Influential Person? Then make sure you are a man or woman of vision. And make sure you get your vision from God, who has a purpose and a plan for each of our lives. When you do, you will be surprised by how many people will get caught up in your flow. Individuals all around us are waiting to be influenced by those who know where they are going and how they plan to get there.

The *V* in VIP stands for Vision! Again, as wise King Solomon said, "Where there is no vision, the people perish" (Proverbs 29:18 KJV).

People who influence
others for good all have
a common characteristic:
they are men and women of
impeccable integrity.

I = Integrity

In a very real sense, being a person of influence is not an option for us. In fact, Paul reminded us, there is an "area of influence God assigned to us" (2 Corinthians 10:13 ESV). Look around you. God has "assigned" you a specific area where your influence for good can make a difference in someone else's life. We have already seen that winsome people who have a lasting influence on those they come into contact with are men and women of vision. They know where they are going, and, even more important, they know how they plan to get there.

Now we uncover the meaning of the *I* in VIP. Some would argue that the *I* should stand for *intellect.* After all, knowledge is power in our modern world. The thinking is that the more we know and the greater expertise we gain in a specific area, the more influence we will have on others. Others would argue that the *I* should represent *intensity*—the spirit of conquest some people possess that is usually accompanied by a passion that becomes contagious. Some men and women have the incredible gift of a persuasive personality and the ability to move and sway crowds with their outstanding oratory. Still others argue that this perpendicular letter in the middle of *VIP* best represents *insight*, meaning good old common sense coupled with the ability to discerningly see through issues and come to proper conclusions.

However, over my decades of observing people and studying leadership and influence traits, I have known highly intelligent men and women who display a keen intellectual knowledge and strong persuasive abilities but who possessed little integrity and therefore have lost their influence. I have known other people who display a powerful intensity for their tasks, an intensity manifested in boundless energy and optimism. They could attract followers like honey attracts bees. But, unfortunately, somewhere along the way, often in money or moral matters, they revealed that they had little integrity, and they lost their influence. The absence of integrity outweighs the presence of insight, and these people lose their influence.

In the final analysis, if both you and I want to become very influential people, the *I* must stand for *integrity.* People who influence others for good all have a common characteristic: they are men and women of impeccable integrity.

Integrity can be defined as "the steadfast and constant adherence to a moral or an ethical code." It is also "the state or quality that strives to be complete, free from the corrupting influences of improper motives and methods." The thesaurus pairs *integrity* with such words as *honesty*, *completeness*, and *incorruptibility*. In the New Testament, *integrity* is translated from a compound Greek word containing a negative prefix, the preposition *through* and the noun *corruption*. The word literally describes a man or woman in whom there runs "no corruption through them." It suggests consistency between what we do in public and who we are in private. That is to say, a person of integrity is in public exactly what he or she is in private.

Integrity causes the professional golfer to turn himself in on a minor infraction when no one else has seen or noticed it. It causes a witness to tell the whole truth on a witness stand when no one else would know if she were less than truthful. Integrity causes employees to refrain from cheating on overtime hours or expense accounts. And integrity should keep us honest when April 15 rolls around and the IRS wants its money. Integrity is what keeps us faithful to our wives and husbands when one of us is away from home on a business trip.

Our contemporary culture is desperately in need of men and women of integrity. Too many of our national leaders from both sides of the political aisle have failed on this count. Too often another gate swings open to reveal someone living with little or no integrity. We have gone from Watergate to

Irangate to Monicagate and on and on. Scandals have too often arisen in some of the nation's highest offices, and our culture is reaping the results of that lack of integrity in leaders who argue about "what the meaning of the word *is* is." No wonder a large part of the populace wonders if character really does count anymore. Electing people with integrity doesn't seem as important to some voters as it once was. But we will never be people with lasting influence for good if we do not live lives of integrity.

Our modern culture is being crippled by a lack of integrity. Too many cities in America, like my own, have seen widespread corruption and investigations of wrongdoing in their school systems and city governments. More than one leader in my city recently resigned from office in disgrace before he would have been publicly exposed or indicted for corruption. Sadly, too many religious leaders score no better in the area of integrity. As I write this very paragraph, I have just heard the tragic news of another high-profile pastor and religious leader who has resigned due to his lack of integrity.

So in terms of integrity, what are you personally doing about the fact that God has assigned to you an "area of influence"? You may be the most visionary person in the world, but if you don't live with integrity, you will join the many others on the ash heap of "what might have been." People who have a lasting legacy of influence have this in common: they are men and women of integrity.

We begin to discover integrity's important role when we realize that each of us simultaneously lives in four very distinct spheres of life and therefore of influence.

You live in a *private world*, that part of your existence where no one else enters. Not even those closest to us—not even our husbands or our wives—know all our private thoughts. No one enters your private world except you . . . and the God who gave you a DNA like no one else's, who searches your heart and who knows all your private thoughts.

You also live in a *personal world*, that sphere of your life you share with only your small circle of immediate family and perhaps a few close friends who know you well. This world consists only of those who know you as you really are . . . behind closed doors.

Next, you also live in a *professional world*, that ever-widening circle of dozens, scores, or, perhaps even a few hundred people who know you in a professional setting. We come into contact with this world every day at work, at school, or in the civic and social arena.

Finally, you live in a *public world*, the widest sphere of influence where people form opinions of us for good or for bad. This world consists of people who do not know us professionally, much less personally, and of course not privately, yet when they hear our name, they have formed an opinion about us. Some often refer to who we are in this world as our public persona.

Keep these four worlds in mind as we consider why so many people seem to live with so little integrity. There have always been people who seek to mask their lack of integrity by attempting to portray a positive public image. However, in the professional world, a lack of integrity becomes a bit more difficult to disguise. Then, when we get home and behind the closed door, it is virtually impossible to keep up the act around those who truly know us. In fact, many parents have lost their kids when those kids see Mom or Dad be one way in the public or professional world, but be someone quite different in a personal setting. Finally, we come to the private world of God Himself and just us—and there is no hiding from Him.

So in which world is our integrity rooted? Some seem to think we root it in the public world, but we don't. Integrity is not rooted in the public world; its presence or absence is only revealed there. Ultimately, our behavior in the public world will reveal for all to see whether or not we are living with integrity.

Some people maintain that integrity is rooted in the professional world where, in our areas of responsibility, we choose whether to live out the principles of integrity in our professional dealings with others. Our integrity, however, is not rooted in the business world, but it can be reinforced there or even undermined there by our dealings with others.

Then there are individuals who insist that integrity must be rooted in the close, interpersonal dynamic of our personal world. That idea seems logical, but integrity is not rooted there. It is simply reflected in our relationships with those who know us best. If you want to know if I have integrity, ask my own wife. After all, she knows me better than anyone else in the world.

By the process of elimination and the principles of logic, integrity is rooted in the private life, that part of us that is alone with God and will live for eternity with Him. When integrity has established strong roots in our private world, it will be reflected in our personal world. Our own family and our closest friends will see the integrity in our personal relationships that flows from our deeper private life. Then, as our influence widens to the professional world, our honest dealings with others—what we say and how we act—will reflect the standard of integrity we choose to live by. And ultimately our integrity will be revealed for God's glory in the public world.

Similar to the development of a vision, integrity is conceived in the private world, birthed in the personal world, grows in the professional world, and matures in the public world.

INTEGRITY IS ROOTED IN OUR PRIVATE LIFE

You've undoubtedly heard architects, engineers, or builders say, "That building has structural integrity." What exactly do they mean by this phrase? These experts are saying that the public beauty and grandeur of a tall, majestic skyscraper reaching up to the heavens stands steady only because the unseen foundation is dug deep into the earth and the infrastructure of the steel beams is solidly constructed. It is the hidden life of a building that gives it structural integrity. It is the hidden life of an orange tree, that unseen root system that spreads out and burrows its way deep into the earth, that produces those juicy and delectable fruits. And so it is with us. Our own integrity must be rooted in our private life, that part of our existence that we spend alone with God in the secret place. Integrity stems from an inner strength, not any outer promotion. Integrity is rooted in the private life we develop when we are alone with God.

At this writing, Billy Graham is in his declining years. It was my personal joy to be called his pastor during my years

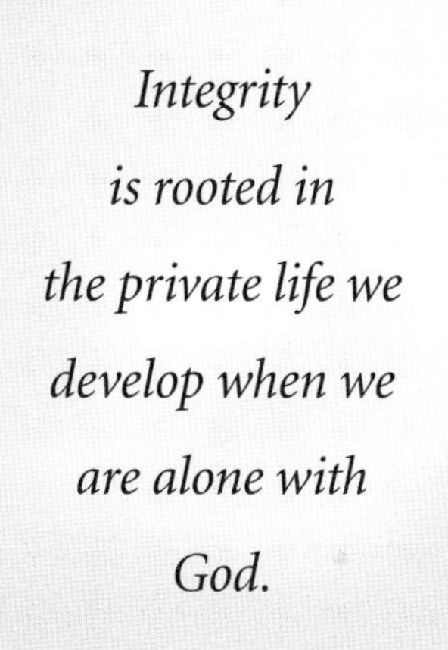

Integrity
is rooted in
the private life we
develop when we
are alone with
God.

of service at First Baptist Church in Dallas where he kept his church membership. What made this man so influential and so trusted by so many across several decades? Scores of times in interviews and on television talk shows he has been asked, "Why you? Why have you had such a worldwide platform? Why have kings and presidents sought your wise counsel?"

I believe that it is not because of what Billy Graham has been in public, preaching to millions of people around the globe. He is respected and consulted because what he has been in private for over three quarters of a century impacts his public persona: his integrity is the single factor that has consistently separated him from so many others. Through the years other pastors or evangelists might have had keener minds or more persuasive speech, but they dropped out of the race. What has made Billy Graham's influence last so long? What made him so influential, so believable and credible through the years? It is neither his intellect nor his intensity; it is his personal integrity rooted in his private life. King Solomon had it right when he said, "The integrity of the upright guides them" (Proverbs 11:3 ESV).

As we've noted before, the exiled Daniel, living in the pagan culture of ancient Babylon, was also a man of integrity who possessed "an excellent spirit" (Daniel 6:3). This simply means that Daniel rooted his life in his private world and that the Spirit of the living God led him in life. Again, what is inside of you gives you integrity, not what is outside of you. Integrity is brought about by the inner choice to live by God's principles, not by outer promotion. So would you use the word *excellent* to describe your spirit? How do you really think of yourself? Do you think of yourself in terms of being a body who just happens to have a spirit-soul within? Many of us today are primarily body conscious: we spend most of our time working on our bodies, not our spirit. We tone them, tan them, and sometimes tuck them. But your body is only the house you are residing in during your earthly pilgrimage. The real you is your spirit within. So how would you describe your spirit?

Remember that integrity is rooted in the private world. If we are primarily body conscious, then self-exaltation easily raises its ugly head in our relationships. Pride exhibited in the personal arena spills into the professional world, and ultimately flows into the public arena. However, if we become spirit conscious, we will root our integrity in our private world so that it ultimately is revealed in the public world for God's glory. We are all spirit beings who are simply living in a body that is deteriorating with every passing day and that will eventually end up as dust. True integrity must be rooted in our spirit, that part of us that is immaterial and the part of us that will live as long as God lives.

A parable Jesus told in the world's greatest sermon paints a picture of this truth. His message is famously known as the Sermon on the Mount and is recorded for all posterity in Matthew 5–7. Jesus concluded this rich sermon with a story about a wise man who had built his home on the foundation of solid rock. He was speaking about a man of integrity. When a listener asked about the meaning of His message, Jesus replied that the wise builder was a man who heard the Word of God and put it into practice in his daily life. Personal integrity, rooted in our private life, is protected and strengthened by our close relationship with Jesus.

INTEGRITY IS REFLECTED IN OUR PERSONAL LIFE

When we root our integrity in the secret and hidden place where we get alone with God, that integrity will soon be reflected in our relationships with those who know us best. Our transparency and integrity will be reflected in our countenance and conduct as we interact and talk with family and friends in our personal world. Those with whom we share life's most personal moments will readily observe our faithfulness to God's standards of honesty and uprightness. Even when the winds of personal pressures, public opinion, or political expediency blow against us, our integrity will be reflected in our personal dealings with those closest to us.

We live in a time of tremendous cultural change, and a buzzword in the Western world is *tolerance*. The word once meant respecting other people's beliefs and truth claims without necessarily accepting them. Today *tolerance* has a new definition in our culture. It now means that all truth claims are valid and should be accepted as such. If all truth claims are valid, we have no moral absolutes, and more often than not that seems to be the case. Relativism is on the march and waving high its flag of tolerance. The personal reality is that we have what we tolerate. What we tolerated yesterday, we have today. Parents can attest to this. Yesterday, for instance, parents who tolerated their children talking back to them, disobeying, and being disrespectful today see their young adults having little to no respect for authority and, too often, being in constant trouble. This pattern of one day having what we tolerate is true in every endeavor of life. Coaches who allow their teams to merely go through the motions of undisciplined and sloppy practices reap what they sow when game day rolls around. What we tolerate today, we will have tomorrow.

Clearly, becoming a very influential person in today's world demands personal integrity. You might be the brightest bulb in the room when it comes to intellect and the most passionate person around when it comes to intensity, but without integrity you will never be a man or woman of influence. Integrity

You might be the brightest bulb in the room when it comes to intellect and the most passionate person around when it comes to intensity, but without integrity you will never be a man or woman of influence.

is rooted in our private world and is reflected in our personal world.

INTEGRITY IS REINFORCED IN OUR PROFESSIONAL LIFE

When it comes to our character and integrity, the world is a pretty poor judge, but it is a very sufficient judge of our conduct. Consider your own professional life, your ever-widening circle of influence, and the arena of life where integrity is revealed more and more. In the marketplace, people with personal integrity find it either reinforced or undermined in their everyday dealings with others. It speaks volumes that one of the biggest challenges for small-business owners today, in an age of entitlement, is finding honest personnel to hire. Many retail outlets are far more concerned about theft from insiders than from outsiders who might shoplift. For too many people, integrity is absent from the marketplace.

It's no wonder that if we have personal integrity it will surface and even stand out in the workplace. The apostle Paul made this crystal clear in his cyclical letter to the Ephesians when he said, "Be obedient to those who are your masters . . . in sincerity of heart, as to Christ" (Ephesians 6:5). Men and women of integrity are characterized in the marketplace by carrying out their assigned tasks. These followers of Christ recognize His authority over all their lives and recognize the authority He has established in sports, on the freeway, in the community, at school, and in government. Why shouldn't we also recognize and respect authority in our professional settings?

In our professional lives, when we show up for work on time and perform our duties with excellence, we are doing what integrity demands and thereby reinforcing what has been rooted in us. The person of integrity realizes that his time on the job is not his own but belongs to his employer. We have no right to use our employer's time, for which we are being compensated, for our own personal endeavors. In fact, when we work inefficiently or tend to personal matters while we're on the job, we are actually stealing from our employer. If we arrive late for work, ease into our day, take extra time for lunch, and extend our break periods beyond the limit, we are as guilty of stealing as the one who takes money from the petty cash drawer.

People with influence are people of integrity who faithfully perform their duties in the professional world. Paul went on to say that we are to work "not with eyeservice, as men-pleasers, but as bondservants of Christ, doing the will of God from the heart" (Ephesians 6:6). Yes, integrity that is rooted in the private life—that is "from the heart"—will not only be reflected in our personal life but reinforced in our professional life as well. The marketplace, not the church, is our biggest opportunity to engage our culture and begin transforming it by the influence of our personal integrity. We are not to be simply "men pleasers"; we aren't to be controlled by the opinions of the people around us. Instead, those of us who want our personal integrity to influence others don't take a poll to determine popular opinions before making our decisions. Why? Because our integrity emanates "from the heart" and is reinforced in the professional setting.

In Paul's discourse on personal integrity in the marketplace, he concluded by stating that we are to do our work "with goodwill doing service, as to the Lord, and not to men" (Ephesians 6:7). People of integrity realize they are serving the Lord whether they work on an assembly line, in a textile mill, behind a computer in a high-rise office building, in a hospital, at home with the children, in a classroom, or behind a big mahogany desk on the top floor. As men and women of integrity, we are to be honest and honorable in our places of employment. Furthermore, working "as to the Lord, and not to men" gives our labor and effort a new dignity. When a waiter serves a customer "as to the Lord," he will do so with a dignity that positively influences his words and actions. When a medical doctor attends to a sick patient "as to the Lord," she will do so with dignity and with respect for the patient.

We will never influence others in the professional world if we are not already people of integrity when we step into that arena. Again, integrity is not rooted in the marketplace, but is only reinforced there. If we ever hope to become a VIP—a person of influence—in the workplace, we can't leave our integrity at home. We need to keep the roots of our integrity strong in our private world so that it will be reflected in our personal world with those who love us most and then naturally characterize our work and be reinforced in our professional world for all to see.

INTEGRITY IS REVEALED IN OUR PUBLIC LIFE

Whenever we are thrust into the public arena, it is too late to start from scratch in an effort to become a person of integrity. Again, we need to already possess it. What we truly are in private will ultimately be revealed in public.

Many of us remember Bible stories from childhood. Some of the most repeated ones have a common thread woven through them: a person got into trouble not because he had done something wrong but because he had done something right! Do you remember Joseph? He once found himself in an Egyptian dungeon. Why? His master's wife tried to seduce him, and when he refused, she accused him of trying to rape her. And what about Daniel? He found himself cast into a den of lions, a fate that should have meant a gruesome death. Why? Because he wouldn't bow down to a golden image and wouldn't bend before the king. Daniel stood on his own inner conviction and commitment to living a life of integrity. In our upside-down world, it is not always true that when we do wrong we will be punished and when we do right we will be rewarded. At times the reverse is true.

But back to Joseph and Daniel. Most of us know the happy endings of both these stories. Joseph was ultimately released and promoted to a place of leadership in the most progressive nation in his time. Daniel was delivered from the lions' den without a scratch. What did these two men have in common? Both lived with a personal integrity that had been rooted in the private world where they nurtured their relationships with God. As illustrated by their lives, the world often notices people of integrity and provides them with a platform of influence beyond their wildest imaginations. Sooner or later integrity—or its absence—is always ultimately revealed in the public world.

So what do twenty-first-century people of integrity face? Our contemporary culture is bringing new challenges to the Christian faith with each passing day and with every new court ruling. Those of us who have adhered to a Judeo-Christian ethic have suddenly found ourselves living in a culture as foreign as Joseph knew in Egypt or Daniel knew in Babylon. Our value systems, the truth we proclaim, and our moral compasses are being strongly challenged. The world has evolved into one of massive pluralism with an ever-encroaching paganism attached to various belief systems. More than ever it is time for men and women of integrity to rise up. Never has the nation—the world—so greatly needed people who root their integrity in their private lives, reflect it in their personal lives, reinforce it in the professional arena, and reveal it for all to see in the public world.

So you want to become a VIP, a very influential person? Others will never get truly caught up in your flow of influence unless you are a person of impeccable integrity and character. Individuals who influence others are people of vision who know where they are going and how they are getting there. They are also people of integrity who know who they are and why they do what they do.

The psalmist Asaph wrote of King David that he lived his life and led his people "according to the integrity of his heart, and guided them by the skillfulness of his hands" (Psalm 78:72). You may be riding high at the top of your class. You may be moving up the ladder of success with one promotion after another. You may even have the personality to charm the most cynical among us. But if you are not a person of integrity, you will falter and fail in the long run. Remember, God has assigned a sphere of influence just to you. VIPs, people with true and lasting influence, are men and women with vision . . . and integrity.

If we are going to influence those in our assigned sphere, we must be people who are moved and motivated by a focused purpose in life.

P = Purpose

Now for the final letter in our acronym. VIPs, those who influence others in life, are people of vision: they know where they are headed and how they plan to arrive at their destinations. VIPs are also people of integrity: they are guided by an inner commitment to integrity that enables them to practice on the outside what they profess to be on the inside. Finally, if we are going to influence those in our assigned sphere, we must be people who are moved and motivated by a focused purpose in life. Each of us has a job to do that we can do like no one else can. It is exciting to live according to the divine plan and the determined purpose of your life.

No one ever had the kind of impact or lasting influence upon generations through the centuries as Jesus of Nazareth. He was a person of vision, He was a person of integrity, and He lived focused on His God-given inner purpose. Consider a conversation He had with His disciples. Once, in the gospels, Jesus was determined to detour from the normal Jewish route while traveling between Galilee and Judea—He felt led to make the journey straight through the region of Samaria. But this was a route a first-century Jew in his right mind did not want to take. It is difficult, if not impossible, to describe the boiling racial and ethnic hatred that permeated the mood of personal animosity and distrust between a first-century Jew and a Samaritan. At one point on their journey, the disciples went into a town to buy food while Jesus waited for them outside the village of Sychar. When the disciples returned, Jesus responded by saying, "My food"—the thing that sustains Me and keeps Me going; My purpose in life—"is to do the will of Him who sent Me, and to finish His work" (John 4:34). Jesus lived with a driving purpose in life as He walked the ways of this world encased in human flesh. It was this purpose-driven life that led Him to the place to which He was ultimately sent—the cross of Calvary.

Jesus knew His purpose for being on this earth. And everything on this earth has a primary purpose. A pen's primary purpose is to write. I would rather have an inexpensive plastic pen that wrote every time I used it than an expensive German one that skipped and left smudges. A car's primary purpose is to take us from one place to another. I would rather have an old car that reliably started every time I turned on the ignition than an expensive new foreign car that started half the time.

What is your primary purpose in life? VIPs—besides being people of vision and integrity—are people with a passion to fulfill their purpose in life.

Sometimes that purpose is reflected on tombstones. I have always found it fascinating to see the epitaphs etched in stone on the graves of those who have gone before us. Those words have a way of telling something about the deceased's personality. Winston Churchill, for instance, was a great world leader with an often caustic nature. You may have heard about the friction between him and Lady Astor, the American-born debutante who married into Britain's upper class. To Churchill's disdain, she became the first female member of the British Parliament. On one occasion when she was annoyed with Churchill, Lady Astor exclaimed, "Sir, if you were my husband, I would give you poison in your tea." Churchill fired right back, saying, "If I were your husband, I would drink it!" His wit extended to his epitaph. When he died in 1965, his final request was that his own tombstone read, "I am ready to meet my Maker. Whether my Maker is prepared for the great ordeal of meeting me is another matter."

Consider a few other revealing examples. As a young man Benjamin Franklin wrote in his diary what he wanted on his tombstone: "The Body of B. Franklin, Printer; like the Cover of an old Book, Its Contents torn out, And stripped of its Lettering and Gilding, Lies here, Food for Worms. But the Work shall not be wholly lost; for it will, as he believed, appear once more, in a new & more perfect Edition, Corrected and amended By the Author." And then there is the epitaph of Mel Blanc, the legendary voice of dozens of Warner Bros. cartoon characters. He chose for his epitaph a signature line he often quoted when voicing Porky Pig: "That's all, folks!"

But no better epitaph could ever be etched in stone than the one the apostle Paul gave to King David: "When David had served God's purpose in his own generation, he fell asleep" (Acts 13:36 NIV). Anyone who has studied the life of King David has seen that he was indeed moved and motivated and, as a result, focused on a single purpose. Therefore no better words could describe his well-lived life than these: "David served God's purpose in his own generation." Could any better words be written on your own tombstone than these? "You served God's purpose in the sphere of influence He assigned to you."

Those people in the Bible who are like David—who live with a driving purpose—have a servant's heart. Think of the many character traits and accomplishments Paul could have commended King David for. David was an amazing motivator of men: when he was fleeing from King Saul, masses of men followed him with unparalleled loyalty. David led Israel to become the world power of his day. He was an incredible fund-raiser: he raised all the money to build the temple in Jerusalem. But when it came time to remember him for all posterity, Paul said, "David served." David knew that the way down—on his knees as a servant—was the way up—to God's approval. When describing King David's servant heart, Paul used a compound Greek word seldom found in the New Testament: a preposition meaning "under" plus a verb meaning "to row." In other words, David was an under rower. Immediately, Paul's audience would have raced to the mental image of those massive Greek wooden sailing vessels with openings down the sides of the hull and large oars emerging from them, driving in and out of the sea. Down below the deck, chained to their seats, were the servants known as under rowers. David didn't lead from on deck all the time, barking orders and commanding others. He was a servant leader who saw himself as an under rower.

During the summer before my senior year in college, this servant attitude came home to my heart. I had come to faith in Christ three years before, and that summer I was preparing to take the LSAT exams for law school when I sensed the call of

God to ministry. I concluded my senior year, graduated with a business administration degree, and then started attending seminary. Frustration set in as I saw so many of my fellow classmates with opportunities to preach, and none were coming my way. My pastor offered some advice that at the time I felt was insensitive. Rather gruffly he spit out a paraphrased scripture to me: "You be faithful over little things, and God will make you ruler over greater things." But I received it. I found a nursing home that let me come and deliver a message once a week. Then I discovered a rescue mission where I weekly preached to those on skid row. My purpose in life drove me to become an under rower myself. That was decades ago, and not a week has passed since that didn't offer me multiple opportunities to preach the gospel. God had called me to be an under rower in His kingdom—and He has blessed me with tremendous opportunities to serve Him.

While David regarded himself as an under rower, it is important to note what David was actually serving. David served "God's purpose." This can be exhilarating. The best way to serve God and those around us is to determine the very purpose for which we were created, the exact purpose for which we exist, and then serve in that capacity. When we do so, this amazing promise from God is ours: "We know that all things work together for good to those who love God, *to those who*

The best way to serve God and those around us is to determine the very purpose for which we were created, the exact purpose for which we exist, and then serve in that capacity.

are called according to His purpose" (Romans 8:28, emphasis mine).

When we focus on serving God by fulfilling our assigned purpose in life, situations and circumstances have—by God's grace and choreography—a way of working together for our good. Looking back over your own journey through life, think about those times that seemed disastrous but actually, in the end, worked out for your good. Yes, things "work together," but not by accident or blind chance. (The Greek word translated "work together for our good" is the same Greek word from which we derive our English word *synergy.*) This certainly does not mean that everything that comes knocking on our door is necessarily good. In fact, many of us are too often confronted with things that are downright bad: there are financial failings, sicknesses, rebellious children, dying marriages, and disappointments ad infinitum. This verse does mean that God can take our mistakes and the messes and misfortunes in our lives and weave them all together into a tapestry of the cross, and He does so for our good and His glory.

But for those of us focused on living according to God's purpose in life, there is more to this promise. Note what the verse says: "*all things* work together for good." Can we really believe this? Had the apostle said "some things" or "many things" or even "most things," the statement would be a bit more palatable. But "all things"? *All things* includes unfair circumstances, unfortunate occurrences, and unfaithful people. As Paul wrote these words, he was basing them on personal experience. He had been shipwrecked at Malta, and he was stoned at Lystra where he was left for dead. He was repeatedly beaten and berated as he traveled on his missionary journeys. He knew firsthand the truth of these words as he pursued his purpose in life with a laser focus.

Yes, for those of us who have found our purpose, "all things" are what? "Working together." For what? "Good." To whom? "To those who are called according to His *purpose*." True VIPs are moved and motivated, driven and directed, by an inner God-given purpose.

This is a good moment to ask a very personal and pointed question: What is your purpose in life?

As you consider your answer, look at your thumb. Go ahead. Take a moment and just look at it. No one alive today has a thumbprint exactly like yours. And what about your deoxyribonucleic acid, that unseen and unique molecule that resides in every cell of your body? You most likely are more familiar with its acronym: DNA. No one alive today—and no one who has ever walked on this planet in all of human history—has DNA exactly like yours. You are a unique and one-of-a-kind individual. There has never been, there is not right now, and there never will be someone like you. And you are indescribably valuable to God. And He has a purpose for your life. Somewhere there is a role on this earth for you to fulfill in a way no one else could. God made you unique for a special purpose. Those who influence others in life—who see others caught up in their flow—are men and women consumed with pursuing their God-given purpose and finishing the work He has given them to do.

Understand there is purpose for your very existence: as the Westminster Catechism puts it, "The chief end of man is to glorify God and enjoy Him forever." God also has a singular purpose for you alone to pursue, and—amazingly—this personal purpose existed before you even drew your first breath. Through the prophet Jeremiah, God said as much: "Before I formed you in the womb I knew you; before you were born I sanctified you" [set you apart from all others] (Jeremiah 1:5). What an awesome thought! *You* have a God-given purpose that has been there all along.

A rather unspiritual experience drove this truth deep into my heart and mind. Now I have never been known for my handyman skills, but when we moved our daughter into her freshman college dorm room, I was assigned the task of assembling a small pedestal table. Only four screws were involved, so how hard could it be? Upon examination I observed that the screws were Phillips head: they had an x instead of one long groove. I knew I needed a Phillips screwdriver, but in my impatience and haste, I grabbed a kitchen knife instead. I pressed it into the screw and worked hard to turn it, but, not surprisingly, I had little, if any, success. My wife went to her toolbox, pulled out a Phillips screwdriver, and, with a frown, tossed it in my direction. That Phillips screwdriver fit those little grooves perfectly—and it felt so satisfying to screw them tight. And I actually began to feel pretty good about myself. What was the difference between my initial failure and my success? I had the right tool: the screwdriver was doing exactly what it was made to do. All that is to say, some of us may not be performing in the sphere of influence God has assigned to us because we have not found our purpose and put it to proper use. It might be time for some of us to stop trying to tighten a Phillips screw with a kitchen knife. It just doesn't work.

Let me reassure you, though, that finding this purpose in life may not be as difficult as it appears. We can learn from Jesus. As the shadows began to fall on Gethsemane's garden, the Lord was in anguish . . . praying . . . passionate about accomplishing His purpose in life. Earlier He had said to His disciples, "I have come down from heaven, not to do My own will, but the will of Him who sent Me" (John 6:38). Now, as the darkness set in on the evening before He would hang on a Roman cross, it was this desire to do God's will that consumed Him. He prayed, "Father, if it is Your will, take this cup away from Me; nevertheless not My will, but Yours, be done" (Luke 22:42). And may that prayer always be yours and mine: "Not my will, but Yours, Father."

God has a purpose and a plan for each and every one of us. David was confident of that: "You will show me the path of life; in Your presence is fullness of joy; at Your right hand are pleasures forevermore" (Psalm 16:11). In fact, the same God who made you unique and different from everyone else is undoubtedly more interested in you finding His purpose than you are. Know that He does not want to veil His purpose from us, but He wants to reveal it to us. There are three important steps to making its discovery.

First, be sure you know the *Savior.* It stands to reason that if we are looking to find our purpose in life, we should first be in relationship with the One who designed us. We can only know God if we have a saving knowledge of Christ (please see the "Conclusion" on page 85). Otherwise a person cannot discern

God's will or purpose because it is "spiritually discerned" (1 Corinthians 2:14). Next, be sure you know the *Spirit*. When we place our trust in Christ, the Holy Spirit takes up residency within us and empowers us to fulfill our purpose. God's Spirit within us is our Guide, and He leads us "into all truth" (John 16:13). Being sensitive to the Spirit's leading in our lives is key to discovering God's purpose for us. Finally, be sure you know the *Scripture*. God will never lead His followers to do anything contrary to what He has taught in His Word. When we know Christ, when we are being led by His Spirit within us, and when we are living according to His Word, He will make known to us "the path of life" (Psalm 16:11). God has a wonderful plan and purpose for your life, and He longs to make His will known to you.

As we have previously noted, no individual has influenced as many people as Jesus Christ has. He possessed a world-changing vision. He was Integrity incarnate. He spoke God's truth, He challenged us to live by it, and He lived out everything He preached. And Jesus' purpose was the driving force behind everything He said and did. I have noticed something about people who understand their purpose: they are moved to do whatever is required of them—and then some. And this passion

When we know Christ, when we are being led by His Spirit within us, and when we are living according to His Word, He will make known to us "the path of life" (Psalm 16:11).

becomes contagious. The phrase "going the second mile" has found its way into our modern vernacular to describe the man or woman who goes beyond what is expected or even required of them to influence others. In Jesus' own words, "Whoever compels you to go one mile, go with him two" (Matthew 5:41).

"Going the second mile" finds its roots in first-century Palestine. The Romans had conquered most of the Mediterranean world. One of the marvels of their conquest was the vast system of superhighways they had built for travel between their conquered territories and Rome. In fact, more than fifty thousand miles of these Roman roads traversed their expanding empire. At the end of every mile on every road was a stone marker that provided direction, warned of potential dangers ahead, and indicated the distance to both the next town and to Rome itself. (This is the source of the phrase "All roads lead to Rome.")

By law, a Roman citizen or soldier could command a subject from one of the conquered provinces to carry his load or backpack for him. However, by law, these Romans could only compel that person to carry it one mile and no more. That backstory sheds light on Jesus' reference to the second mile in His Sermon on the Mount. Having sat on the very spot on the northern shore of the Sea of Galilee where He spoke these words, I have wondered if this lesson was not unfolding before

Him as He spoke. I can almost see Him stop and point His hearers to a Roman soldier grabbing some young man from the crowd and handing him his backpack to carry. At this point, I imagine, Jesus would have said, "Whoever compels you to go one mile, go with him two!"

Can you imagine what this sounded like to those people oppressed and beaten down by the Roman occupation? In spite of the animosity and even resentment they undoubtedly felt, Jesus was calling upon them to do not only what the law required of them, but more.

Doing more than what is required—isn't that what sets some people apart in athletics, or education, or business, or the arts, or, for that matter, any endeavor? This drive, this inner purpose, moves and motivates certain people to do more than what is required or expected. The second mile Jesus commanded is not only one of the secrets to success in life but also a VIP attitude that influences others.

Back to our miles. Jesus referred to two miles. The first is what one might call the mandated mile, and it is a matter of necessity. The second is a miracle mile, fueled by an inner purpose and perhaps having a lasting influence on people around us.

The mandated mile—established by law—is often accepted as a given in Jesus' story. In fact, I never remember reading an article or hearing much about this first mile, only about the second. But the first mile represents that which is required of us, and that one is always the hardest. Ask any distance runner. No runner's high has been reached and no second wind ever kicks in during the first mile. Besides, it is usually not as easy to enjoy the things we know we have to do as it is to enjoy the things we want to do.

Being a VIP has its own first mile on which it is often tough to get started. Any first-century Jew, living under the iron hand of Roman rule, would tell you as much. The first mile interrupts your schedule. It can take you away from people you love, projects you were working on, and work that paid the bills. That first mile not only calls upon you to bear a burden that belongs to someone else, but you also have to be willing to swallow your own pride as you walk that mile. Likewise, the most difficult part of becoming a person of influence comes with getting started on this first mile, a truth that applies to almost every discipline of life. The hardest part about a regular exercise program is getting started. Similarly, for me, getting started on a diet is more difficult than keeping it going. Many believers know it would be good to memorize more Scripture, but never seem to because of this very fact. We cannot play leapfrog with

Jesus' words about the second mile. We need to acknowledge that we can't enjoy the second mile unless we endure the first one.

Once we have completed the first mile, we may discover that taking the second one is a very different experience from the first. This miracle mile is not motivated by some law, but instead by our love for Christ: we are serving this person because we love Jesus, not the owner of the backpack. It is our going this second mile that truly influences people; they see us living out an inner purpose in the sphere of influence God has assigned us. Going this second mile also has a way of brightening our road. Think about it. Imagine a first-century young man busy at his trade. Try to get inside his skin for a moment. Here comes a tall, muscular Roman soldier, clad head to toe in the regalia of his crimson uniform, complete with breastplate and sword. He calls to the boy and motions for him to stop what he is doing, pick up his backpack, and carry it a mile up the road. This inconvenience will interrupt his day and takes him away from his assigned task. But he has no choice in the matter. The boy must carry the backpack, so he does. But what the soldier doesn't know is this is a second-miler.

After a time, as they approach the one-mile marker, the young man does something the soldier has never seen before. Instead of throwing down the heavy load, spitting on the ground, and heading back in the direction from which he came, he willingly volunteers to go an extra mile with the soldier. Along the way, the boy strikes up a conversation. He pleasantly inquires about life back in Rome and the soldier's family awaiting him there. The soldier is completely baffled by the young man's winsome ways and puzzled by why he's still carrying the backpack. I have often wondered if that Roman soldier at the foot of the cross who proclaimed, "Truly this was the Son of God!" had been earlier influenced by a purpose-driven, second-mile follower of Christ (Matthew 27:54).

Do you see that we cannot travel this second mile without influencing others? It only takes one second-miler going above and beyond the call of duty in a home to positively influence the environment. The same is true at the office, on the athletic team, in the classroom, around the neighborhood, and anywhere else we second-milers find ourselves.

It is important to note this second mile is the mile our Lord Himself, who clearly knew the purpose for which He had come to this planet, walked. Driven by His own purpose for which He was sent, He knew this pathway well. Jesus journeyed that first mile when, according to the plan that had been in place before time began, He stepped out of heaven and into human flesh. He walked that mandated mile compelled by God the Father. Then, during His tenure on this earth, Jesus kept every detail of God's written law. But Jesus didn't stop there: motivated by His love for us, He walked the second mile. He who spoke the planets into existence and placed them in their orbits to run with clocklike precision, He who formed and fashioned each of us, said, "I love you, and I will walk with you." But we went our own way.

It was love that drove Jesus to walk that second mile. His decision to go the second mile took Him to the cross where He bore the weight not of a Roman soldier's load but of our sin, the sin of all humanity, past, present, and future. And with that act—with Jesus' death and resurrection—the process began: somebody told somebody . . . and that somebody told somebody else . . . and somebody else told Johnny Keeton . . . and Johnny Keeton told me when I was seventeen years old. As I type these words, I am still not what I ought to be, but I have never been the same since that day.

What are you doing about the fact that in addition to loving God, enjoying Him, and loving others, there is at any given time a specific purpose for you in life, a specific place God wants you to be serving? Remember, there is no one like you. No one has a thumbprint like yours. No one has DNA like yours. And God has assigned an "area of influence" to you.

VIPs are very influential people. They are led by *vision* that they make sure they get from God. They live with *integrity* that they make sure is rooted in the secret place of their private lives. And down in the very core of their being, they are moved and motivated by an inner *purpose.* And the result of vision, integrity, and purpose? Others get caught up in their flow.

"May He grant you according to your heart's desire, and fulfill all your *purpose*" (Psalm 20:4, emphasis mine).

Right now—no matter who you are, where you are from, or what you have done—you can begin the great adventure for which God created you. . . . It will take vision, integrity, and purpose.

CONCLUSION

I am a golfer, and I have been since my boyhood days when I played the old nine-hole Sycamore Golf Course in Fort Worth. I enjoy the challenges golf brings, but I especially enjoy the opportunities golf affords me to spend four uninterrupted hours with friends or family.

Whenever I'm on the course, I get excited when I arrive at the par threes. Oh, the par fives and the longer par fours give you the chance to show off your powerful long drives, but it is the par threes I love the best. The reason is that it only takes one really good shot out of three to make par. Think about it. You can hit a great tee shot onto the green a few feet from the hole. You can miss a short birdie putt and still make an easy par. Or you can top the ball just a few yards in front of the tee, then hit a brilliant second shot near the hole, and walk off with a short tap-in putt for an easy par. You can even hit a wicked slice or hook off the tee, land nowhere near the green, then hit a second shot that barely makes it onto the green, and finish by sinking a long, winding thirty-foot putt for par. The next time you stand at the tee of a par three, remember this fact: it only takes one really good shot to make par.

Unfortunately, one good shot out of three doesn't work when it comes to being a VIP. All three shots have to be on the money. You can have vision—the ability to see what few can see—but if you do not have integrity, you will not see many people caught up in your flow. You can be a person of impeccable integrity, but if you have little idea of where you are headed in life, much less a driving purpose that moves and motivates you, not many will follow you. You might even be highly driven by a powerful inner purpose, but if you live with a lack of integrity, you will not be an influencer to the degree you could have been. Unlike the par threes in golf, being a true VIP—a very influential person—requires all three shots to be on the mark: vision, integrity, and purpose.

You are reading these words because of the lasting influence of the Lord Jesus Christ in whose flow I was personally caught up as a seventeen-year-old young man. I have been carried away in it ever since. No one has ever left the kind of loving legacy or had the incredible far-reaching influence that Jesus has. He is the ultimate VIP. Jesus is a person of VISION: He calls us to go into the whole world and preach His gospel of love, forgiveness, and eternal life to every single person in every single generation. Now *that* is a vision! And for more than two millennia, men and women have been adopting this vision as their own. Jesus is a person of INTEGRITY: He not only preached the world's greatest sermons and taught the world's most profound life lessons, but unlike every other preacher and teacher who has walked this planet, Jesus perfectly obeyed every single command and lived according to every life lesson that came out of His mouth. Jesus is a person of PURPOSE: He was moved and motivated, driven and directed, by the single compelling purpose to do not His own will but the will of the Father who sent Him. That purpose eventually led Him to a Roman cross outside the city walls of Jerusalem. There He bore the sins of the world, dying our death so we could live His life and taking our sin so we could take His righteousness.

We also have the influence of our New Testament because of the influence Jesus Christ had on those early believers. After getting caught up in Jesus' flow, the apostle Paul influenced the entire Roman world in one generation. Paul was a person of unparalleled VISION: "I press toward the goal for the prize of the upward call of God in Christ Jesus" (Philippians 3:14). The Greek word he chose to describe this goal is *scope* in English.

Like the crosshairs in the scope of a rifle, Paul's vision kept him focused. As a VIP, Paul was also a man of INTEGRITY. To the Corinthians he said, "Our boasting is this: the testimony of our conscience that we conducted ourselves in the world in simplicity and godly sincerity, not with fleshly wisdom but by the grace of God, and more abundantly toward you" (2 Corinthians 1:12). And Paul's entire life was guided by a single PURPOSE. Hear him saying to the Philippians, "This one thing I do . . . I press toward the mark for the prize of the high calling of God in Christ Jesus" (Philippians 3:13–14 KJV).

You and I are no different from those who have gone before us, caught up in the flow of the gospel truth about Jesus. Know that God has something for you to do that no one else can do quite like you can. There is someone you can influence that no one else can influence quite like you can. Remember, we are to "boast only with regard to the area of influence God assigned to us," and He desires that "our area of influence among you may be greatly enlarged" (2 Corinthians 10:13, 15 ESV). God has assigned a specific sphere of influence for *you*! You can become a VIP.

Several years ago my wife, Susie, and I found ourselves at one of those great intersections of life that required a major family decision. At the time we were in Israel. One morning, shortly after sunrise, we were sitting on a rock in a private garden adjacent to the Garden of Gethsemane, praying together. As Susie prayed, I looked down and—to my amazement—I saw at my feet several small diamonds clinging to a single blade of grass. Instinctively, I reached down and plucked the blade of grass to bring it closer to my eyes. Of course they were not diamonds at all, but little droplets of dew that were glistening brightly in the Middle Eastern morning sun. Immediately, a verse of Scripture came in my mind that I had memorized dozens of years earlier but had really not thought about since. It is an obscure verse from the writings of the prophet Hosea. Why I ever memorized it remains a mystery; perhaps I had heard a sermon or studied a teaching on that particular chapter. Regardless, Hosea 14:5 flooded my mind and heart. It is a promise from God to His people—"I will be like the dew to [my people] Israel."

I stared again at those drops of dew on that single blade of grass. God promised to be like those drops of dew to His people. What could that possibly mean? Where does dew come from? We walk outside to get the morning paper and see dew all over the yard. Where does it come from? Does it rise? Does it fall? The answer is . . . neither! Dew simply appears when certain conditions are right. It just shows up. We call it condensation.

So what is God's promise to you and to me in Hosea 14:5? When certain conditions are right in our lives, He shows up just as the dew does.

Our influence happens in the same way: when certain conditions are right in our own lives, we can by God's grace become VIPs, very influential people. When we have a VISION that God sowed and grew in our hearts, when we live with INTEGRITY that is rooted in our relationship with God, and when, down in the very core of our being, we are guided by a single good and God-given PURPOSE that keeps us on track, we will begin to see others getting caught up in our flow. Yes, *you* can become a VIP, a Very Influential Person.

THE BOTTOM LINE

As we have previously noted, no one has a thumbprint like yours. No one has DNA just like yours. You are a unique and special creation. There is no one like you. And right now—no matter who you are, where you are from, or what you have done—*you* can begin the great adventure for which God created you. Yes, it will take vision, integrity, and purpose.

Vision. Before the seed of a vision can be planted, you—like Simon Peter—need to understand that even now God sees you not for who you are, but for who you can become. The Lord has a purpose and a plan for your life, and His plan is that you come to know Him personally by placing your faith in Him and in Him alone. Forgiveness, grace, His love, and heaven are God's gifts to you; they cannot be earned or deserved. Yes, we all are sinners who have fallen short of God's perfect standards for our lives. He is a God of love who does not want to punish us for our sins, but He is also a God of justice and must punish sin. This is where Jesus Christ steps in. Jesus is the God-man who came to earth to take our sins into His own body on the cross. Jesus became sin for us "that we might become the righteousness of God in Him" (2 Corinthians 5:21). And the good news is this: Jesus loves you and has a wonderful plan for your life.

Integrity. The dictionary defines *integrity* as "the quality of being honest; the state of being whole." Wholeness comes when we fill the God-shaped void in our lives. Perhaps you have spent a lifetime seeking to fill this void with things or activities when the something you think you need is actually Someone! The Bible says, "Whoever calls on the name of the LORD shall be saved" (Romans 10:13). While a single prayer does not and cannot save you—God honoring your faith in Jesus as His Son saves you—the following prayer may well express the desires of your heart. If so, simply pray these words in your heart, talking to Jesus as you would talk to a friend:

Dear Lord Jesus, I know I have sinned and do not deserve eternal life. Thank You for taking my sin and dying on the cross for me. Please forgive me for my sin. I want to live my life with You as my Lord and ask You to come into my life right now. I turn to You and place all my trust in You for my salvation. I accept Your gifts of eternal life and forgiveness. Thank You for coming into my life.

If this prayer represents the desires of your heart, these words, spoken by Jesus, are a promise for you: "Most assuredly, I say to you, he who believes in Me has everlasting life" (John 6:47).

Purpose. Now you are ready to begin the great adventure, filled with purpose, of following Jesus into the roles for which He created you in the first place. From now on you can join the Lord Jesus in praying His purpose-filled prayer, "Not my will, but Yours be done!"

Your "area of influence God has assigned" to you is just waiting for you to become a VIP.

EPILOGUE

My Most Unforgettable VIPs (Very Influential People)

Much of what makes each of us who we are today is the people whose paths we have crossed through life and the influence they have had upon us. As I look back over the decades of my own life, I have been caught up in the flow of many men and women who have made an indelible impact on my life and whom God used to form and fashion me into who and what I am today. First this disclaimer: if I wrote just one paragraph about each and every person who has influenced me over the course of my life, this volume would be a long, long read. So, acknowledging that space does not permit me to mention all these folks, I will mention a few and tell their stories with the hope and prayer that someday someone will talk about how they were caught up in your flow in the same manner.

MY MOM AND DAD

For me, home was a happy and secure place. My boyhood was characterized by a very important factor: my parents' presence. They were always there.

I am an only child, born to my mom and dad when they had given up any hope of being able to conceive a child. They were already forty years of age, had been married almost twenty years, and had long since stopped thinking about being parents . . . when I miraculously appeared upon the scene. I am sure it was not a virgin birth, but it was a miracle just the same. They sacrificed so much for me. My dad worked in a lower-level job for the city government all his life on a small salary, holding out for a pension that, in the end, was never enough. I don't know how they always did it, but if it was baseball season, my glove was just as nice and new as any kid's on the team. During track season my spikes were as new and shiny as anyone's. From Little League on, I don't remember my dad and mom ever missing an athletic event of mine. They were always in the stands.

There was one constant in my life: they were there . . . always. I never remember my mom buying a blouse, a skirt, a dress, or anything for herself. Twice a year there would arrive at our home a large parcel from West Texas where my great-aunt lived. The clothes she no longer wore she sent to my mom, and she wore them proudly. Words could never describe how much they sacrificed for me.

All my young life I aspired to be a lawyer. As a boy, I rode the bus downtown and sat in the courtrooms for hours listening to trials. Knowing that my folks would never be able to adequately help with college and law school tuitions I began working two jobs after school and on weekends during my high school years. Those jobs meant I needed a car to go from school to work to home. My dad acquiesced, and I got a 1956 Chevrolet. It was almost ten years old at the time, but it was new to me. We put fifty dollars cash down on that car and financed the remaining $200.00 at the Poly State Bank.

When I brought that car home, my dad set down a basic rule. I could not leave the house without answering these four questions: *Where are you going? Who are you going with? What are you going to do? When will you be home?* Having to answer those questions all the time really irritated me, but—although I didn't admit it at the time—I was really glad he cared.

One Friday night, after dropping off all our dates, my buddies and I met at the local high school hangout for a soda. It was a barbecue joint with a large awning that stretched all the way across the parking lot on the front side of the establishment. You would park under the awning and waitresses, called "car hops," would come out, take your order, then bring your food and drink on an aluminum tray and attach it to your car door and window. We had parked on the far end and were standing outside our cars drinking cokes when, all of a sudden, I saw my dad drive into the parking lot. Fortunately, he didn't see me and parked at the other end of the long awning. My mind was racing. *Why is he here?* I never remembered seeing him eat out at all, and he was never out past 9:00 p.m. unless we had gone into extra innings in a baseball game. I noted the time, and then I knew precisely why he was there. I was supposed to have been home almost an hour earlier.

I watched my dad emerge from his car. Just about the time he walked to the front of it, he spotted me across the way. Have you ever noted how an F-16 fighter pilot locks on a target before he drops his bomb? Our eyes locked. He stared. My heart raced. Then . . . he looked down at the wristwatch on his arm, glared at it a moment, and then looked back to me. Then he got back into his car and drove off—but *I beat him home*! Why? I feared my dad. Oh, at the time, I was a strong teenager and he was around sixty years of age. I didn't fear him physically. What I feared that night—and all my life, for that matter, until I held his hand when he breathed his last breath at ninety-five years of age—was, after all he had done for me, all he had sacrificed for me, that I would do anything to dishonor or displease my dad.

Much of what I am today is because of my mom and dad, who loved me unconditionally, who were always there for me, and who constantly told me I could do anything in life I wanted to do. I wish I could stand at my dad's chair and tell him just one more time where I was going . . . who I was going with . . . what I was going to do . . . and when I would be coming home!

THE BROCKETTS

First let me say, I never once heard the first names of these dear people. They were already well up in years when I first met them. They lived in a small crackerbox house a few doors up the street on my block and directly across from the old vacant lot. As a kid, I played thousands of ball games on that old lot. It was like Yankee Stadium to my pals on Crenshaw Street and me. The only conversation I remember having with Mr. and Mrs. Brockett was when one of us hit a towering fly ball straight through their living room window. I was assigned to go over and apologize and to make certain I retrieved the ball. Since I didn't grow up in church (my folks were moral people, but not church people until after my conversion when they both came to the Lord and served Him with faithfulness and fervor the remainder of their days), we played a lot of our games on Sunday mornings. I would see the Brocketts pull out of their driveway about 9:00 a.m. and return after noon. The process was always repeated on Sunday nights. I didn't know it then, but they were pillars of their church.

Life went on for me. Elementary school turned into junior high, then high school was followed by college and seminary. I had long since moved away from the old neighborhood. Some years later, though, I was preaching in Fort Worth. To announce the event, the church placed an ad in the local newspaper with my name and my picture. After the service that night, I was greeting several people near the front of the auditorium when a very aged and quite feeble little couple came up to me inquiring if I was the same little "Hawkins kid" who grew up on Crenshaw Street. When I affirmed I was that very one, they warmly said, "We are the Brocketts." Then, through tears, they said, "We used to sit at our kitchen table, look out the window at the lot across the street, see you playing ball there, and pause to pray for you before each meal. We never knew what happened to you, and we just came because we wondered if you were that same little boy."

It just might be that those who influence us most in life are people we never have imagined even being very aware of us. Some of these influences we will not know about this side of heaven.

AVA WHITE

It was the 1960s—and what a time to be in high school! Those were the days of pep rallies and pom-poms, glasspack mufflers and drag races, Bass Weejuns and Levis, madras windbreakers and button-down collars, hayrides and sock hops, the Beatles and high school English! When it came time to do my English homework, I would much rather have been, in the words of Petula Clark, "downtown where all the lights are bright." My English teacher's name was Miss Ava White. Emphasis on the "Miss," if you please. Not "Mrs." or "Ms." but "Miss." Miss White had devoted her life to teaching high school English and literature, and along the way she had earned quite a reputation for being a strict, no-nonsense disciplinarian.

The first few weeks in her class, I never really applied myself. I seldom studied because I told myself I was working after school and on weekends and maintaining an active social life. So I was just seeking to get by in her class until at the end of class one day, she announced that she wanted to see me at her desk after the others left.

Immediately, I thought, *I know what this means. She is going to give me a piece of her mind for my conduct and poor grades and, most likely, present me with a pink slip that means a trip to the vice principal's office.* I had been there before. By the way, those were the good old days before corporal punishment was banned from schools and when the idea that my parents would side with me over the principal or the teacher was unheard of!

When everyone had left, Miss White called me to her desk, looked me squarely in the eyes, and said, "Son, you have character. You are smart and entirely capable of doing far better work than you are doing. I simply want you to know I believe in you and am confident you could become an A student if you applied yourself." I couldn't believe what was coming out of her mouth. Miss Ava White believed in me! And her encouraging words—that simple pat on the back—did more for me than I could ever describe. We began to meet together after school. She taught me how to outline and to think more analytically. She believed in me and let me know it. In no time my grades soared. To this very day, decades later, every time I outline a new book or write a new chapter I am indebted to Miss Ava White. She changed the way I thought about myself with a word of affirmation, a simple pat on the back.

Someone you know is just waiting for you to speak to them a positive word, a simple word of affirmation. You might be surprised how many more people would get caught up in your flow if you offered pats on the back!

JOHNNY KEETON

Had it not been for Johnny Keeton, I wonder if I ever would have preached a sermon or written a book.

We were seventeen years of age, and we were going to different high schools in our city. I had not seen Johnny in a year or so, but I knew he went to the same places I did and participated in the same things I did—which, by the way, don't bear repeating in a volume like this.

It was a cold January night during my senior year in high school. After a basketball game I was walking out of the gymnasium and across the parking lot to my car when I heard a familiar voice call my name. I turned around, and it was my old buddy, Johnny. He began to tell me how radically his life had been transformed by his coming to faith in Jesus Christ. I could not believe my ears, much less his boldness, as he talked about a subject I thought was confined within the four walls of some high-steepled, stained-glass church somewhere. But I couldn't stop thinking about what Johnny said that night.

He came by my house the next day and shared more with me about the fact that God loved me and had a wonderful plan for my life. Me? I could count on the fingers of one hand how many times I had been inside a church building. Johnny went on to show me in a pocket-sized New Testament that the Bible says we are all sinners, we cannot save ourselves, and Jesus came to earth to take our sins and pay the death penalty we deserved when He died on the cross. And, Johnny explained, if I chose to believe Jesus is God's Son and place my trust in Christ alone for salvation, I could be forgiven. And Johnny closed with the fact that if I did these things, Christ would take up residency in my heart and never leave me. This good news seemed far too good to be true.

The next Sunday morning Johnny picked me up and took me to the Sagamore Hill Baptist Church. There, for the first time, I heard the gospel preached from a pulpit, and on that cold January morning in 1965, I opened my heart and life to Him. I am not what I ought to be today, but I have never been the same since that day!

On the following Monday evening, Johnny took me to see another high school student, and I watched as Johnny led him to faith also. This incredible young man was the single most committed-to-Jesus teenager I had ever known. I am eternally grateful that I got caught up in his flow in an old parking lot one January night so long ago. And because of Johnny, I developed lifelong relationships with a wonderful group of guys, Mike Rigby and Phil Hoskins among them.

W. FRED SWANK and W. A. CRISWELL

Fred Swank came into my life when I was seventeen, and he has been with me ever since—even though he has been in heaven for over thirty years now. He was my "father in the ministry," and I learned far more from him by watching how he lived than I ever did by listening to his counsel, wise as it always was. He taught me that the ministry—that life itself—is all about people and relationships. It was this giant in my life who encouraged me to never use my people to build my own ministry but to use the ministry I had received from the Lord to build up my people. He was pastor of the Sagamore Hill Baptist Church in Fort Worth for over forty-three years, and he left a legacy of over one hundred young men, like myself, who went out from that single church to serve in full-time, vocational ministry all over the world.

After Dr. Swank died in 1982, I was adopted by W. A. Criswell, who through the years truly became like a father to me. For fifty years this legendary and world-famed leader pastored the First Baptist Church in Dallas. Later, it became one of the joys of my life to succeed him in that historic pulpit. Watching the way he died in his declining years while being cared for by his friend, Jack Pogue, was one of the defining moments of my life. As life and consciousness began to slip away from him, he would often wake Jack in the middle of the night preaching powerfully in his slumber. And when folks would come by to visit him, he would ask, "Oh, have you come for the revival?" He died as he had lived: full of Christ. One of the single joys of my life was delivering his funeral message.

These influential spiritual leaders in my life have been joined by a host of other, older, influential friends in ministry who have stuck "closer than brothers." The list of my "big older brothers" is far too long to place here, but it includes the likes of John Wood, Jerry Vines, Adrian Rogers, Robert Naylor, Roy Fish, Richard Jackson, Paige Patterson, Jack Taylor, R. T. Kendall, Tom Elliff, Jerry Falwell, David Jeremiah, George Sweeting, Gary Frazier, and on and on it goes. My closest brother in ministry is David Hamilton, in whose flow I am forever navigating the rivers of life. He was my constant and consistent partner, by my side in Oklahoma, throughout all the Florida years, and finally back in the concrete canyons of downtown Dallas at First Baptist Church. If ever there was the "real deal," it is David and his wife, Charlotte.

JACK GRAHAM

If you are reading this and have never had a best friend, I cannot really imagine your situation. Jack has been my best friend for fifty years now. We met as teenagers, both young "preacher boys"; we were ordained to the ministry on the same night; and we married our wives the same summer. Like a rose bush in a cyclone fence, our lives have been intertwined since the first day we met. In the late sixties we preached together in the rescue missions and downtown streets of Fort Worth. In the seventies we both pastored churches in Oklahoma not many miles apart. In the eighties I was pastor of First Baptist Church in Fort Lauderdale, and Jack was just thirty miles away at the First Baptist Church in West Palm Beach. Then, since the early nineties, we have both been back in Texas ministering in the city of Dallas. Hardly a day has gone by when we haven't been together or talked on the phone.

Although we didn't know what to call it back then as teenagers, we became—and have remained—accountability partners throughout life's journey. We promised God and each other that we would help each other to stay above the fray of the many things that can destroy a man and a ministry. Jack's reputation has remained spotless, and his character is still beyond reproach. Apart from my immediate family, no one knows me better or loves me more than he does. Everyone needs a best friend like Jack. To get caught up in his flow means you'd better be ready to ride some fast currents.

GENE SMYERS

He was there that cold January day when I came to know the Lord. I was seventeen, and he was in his midthirties. This successful businessman and dedicated churchman became the closest thing I ever had to a big brother. Everyone in our city knew him or knew about him. We shared so many things together, not the least of which was our love for our alma mater,

TCU, and especially our football team. Gene became my mentor in the strongest sense of the word and was one of the greatest influencers in my life. Until his recent death, I never made a major decision in life for which I didn't seek his counsel.

Gene is one of those irreplaceable mentors of life, but since his passing, many of my GuideStone family have helped to fill his void. I have been blessed with incredible trustees and staff through the years. Marcia Will has been a daily influence on me serving as my Administrative Assistant for about twenty-five years now. And John Jones, our COO, has been the greatest fellow worker anyone could have. For two decades we have shared this ministry and made decisions together. He is among the most influential and trusted men in my life today.

SID SPEARS

As a pastor for over a quarter of a century, I could mention innumerable laymen in the church who influenced me in uncountable ways. Sid Spears represents them all. I was the young, twenty-seven-year-old pastor of the First Baptist Church in Ada, and this seventy-year-old oil man and rancher was the chairman of our deacons. He was as full of wisdom and good old "common horse sense" (his term) as anyone I have ever met.

At one point in my tenure, a man in the church was causing so much dissension that I had had my fill of it. I phoned Sid to tell him I was coming by to pick him up; we were going to confront this man. Sid replied, "Now, Preacher, I was out checking the wells early this morning, and I came across a cow paddy all crusted over on the ground. Preacher, it didn't stink at all until I kicked it." Well, that was the end of that conversation, and, like most issues, the one at hand simply passed away . . . quite literally, I might add! Come to think of it, most of the things in my life that I spent time worrying about never even happened.

Today it is my good fortune to have one of Sid's nephews as a close and trusted friend. Dr. Bill Spears, his uncle's favorite, is a chip off the old block and one whose counsel I highly value. Many other laypeople—like Charlie Thompson, Pete and Francis Cantrell, Jim and Sue Scrivner—held up my arms and supported me along the way. I wish space allowed me to mention so many more.

GENE WHIDDON

Few men have influenced my life like this gentle giant of a man, the backbone of our church in Fort Lauderdale and the leading citizen in the city. Mayors, governors, even presidents often sought his wise counsel. For fifteen years we shared breakfast together early every Sunday morning and several other times during the week. It was his vision and leadership that really brought about the incredible worship facilities that the church has today. I can still hear him saying, "O. S., the way to have a good idea is to have lots of ideas."

Gene died like he lived: looking forward. The night before his death, while I was visiting him in his hospital room, I read to him from the Bible about the great marriage supper in heaven when God and man sit down together at this feast. As I left the room and looked back at him, he smiled and said, "I will save you a place at the table." Those were the last words I heard him speak, and the next morning he died, literally in my arms. I will forever be caught up in his flow. His legacy lives on in the lives of his two fine sons, Gene and Scott. If space permitted, I would also speak of Grace Chavis, Bob Hudson, Paul May, and so many more in whose flow I was swept away during those Florida years.

MICHAEL CARDONE

Mike and Francis Cardone entered our lives shortly after our arrival in Fort Lauderdale. We became like a part of their family, and they introduced us to an entirely new Italian culture. They also showed us what Christ can do in the lives of two people whose primary purpose in life is to honor Him. This couple began an automotive parts rebuilding company in the basement of a row house in Philadelphia and grew it into the world's largest privately owned remanufacturer. I can still hear Mr. Cardone saying to me, "It is *written*," always emphasizing the fact that written reports and holding those on your team accountable are vital to success. The Cardones' passion for their workers and their families was only exceeded by their passion for the Lord. There never lived a more dedicated and dynamic couple who became Christ's hand extended to others in need.

The Cardones have long since moved to their heavenly reward, but their vision is still being reproduced by their son Michael in ways that would have exceeded their most optimistic expectations. Today, still family-owned, the company has over five thousand employees, and their products are stocked in every auto parts store in the US and Canada as well as around the world. Michael and his wife, Jacquie, are two of our most encouraging friends, and they are making a difference for Christ in the marketplace like no one else I know. It was a happy day when Susie and I got caught up in the Cardone flow, which moves along the rivers of life with impeccable integrity.

JACK and GARRY KINDER

No doubt many of you reading this book can also attest to the influence of this dynamic duo. It was one of my most fortunate days when these two brothers entered my life. For decades they have been movers and shakers in the insurance field worldwide. They were there when baseball chapel had its beginnings. Jack was one of my very closest friends and the most positive, can-do person you could ever know. He opened a whole new world to me, and even though he is no longer with us, I feel his presence and encouragement every single day. Garry is leaving a lasting legacy through the ministry we now know as Roaring Lambs, teaching people to roar for Christ out in the marketplace, beyond the four walls of the church. It was through Jack and Garry that I met Roger Staubach, whom today I count not only as a close personal friend but one of the greatest men I have ever known.

Lifelong friends are a gift, but throughout life I have learned that there's a real hidden treasure in the discipline of making new friends. Lately I have come to know and love a wonderful group of golfing buddies in the Texas Hill Country who are too numerous to mention. When Al Jaksa introduced me to Duke Covert it was a happy day for me. It was Duke who commented on how amazing it is to meet someone in your sixth decade of life and feel as though you've been best friends forever. Such is life—it really is all about relationships and influence.

KEN COOPER

Any book about people of influence will include Dr. Ken Cooper of aerobics and wellness fame. Count me among the multiplied thousands who are enjoying a healthier and more productive life because of his tireless efforts. He became my personal physician over thirty years ago, and my visit to his office for my annual checkup is the most guarded date on my calendar. Like all influencers, Dr. Cooper practices what he preaches, and at this writing, although he is now in his eighties, he is at the top of his game. The only time any friction has arisen is when Susie and I are dining out, Ken and Millie walk in, and I get worried about what is on my plate! In all seriousness, he caught my cancer in its early stages several years ago, and for that I will be ever grateful.

DAVID AMAD, ZALLI JAFFE, and BRUCE RAMER

Susie and I have journeyed to the Middle East scores of times in our lifetime. Israel is like a second home to us in many ways. It was there that we found common roots with these three incredible friends.

David Amad is my Palestinian brother. Born in Jerusalem, a refugee during the War of Independence, adopted as a young lad by a Texas preacher, raised and educated in Texas, a hugely successful businessman and entrepreneur, and now back in the Middle East, this unforgettable man is absolutely one of the most significant influencers in my life. When we met a quarter of a century ago, it was an instant connection. I have watched this man put into action his great love for his wife, Rima, his kids, his employees, and anyone who touches his life. David is the one person I would call if I needed anything, and I have no doubt he would be at my side in an instant.

Zalli Jaffe, what can I say about you, the most connected man I have ever known! Long years ago, another influencer in my life, Graham Lacey, taught me that I was only three people away from anyone in the world I wanted to reach. Think about it. You know someone who knows someone who knows someone. Life is all about relationships. On countless Shabbat evenings, Susie and I have found ourselves at the table of Zalli and Tamar in Jerusalem. Susie calls it "Tamar's Table," and there we have met so many leaders of Israeli government, politics, and business who, across the years, have become dear and trusted friends. We think of them every Friday night and long for the next time we will sit with them again in their Holy City.

Have you ever met someone and instantly known they would become close and dear friends? So it was the first time I met Bruce Ramer and his wife, Madeline. We were about to board a flight in Tel Aviv, and I only wish time and space permitted to tell the details of that eventful evening. Bruce is one of the world's leading entertainment lawyers with offices on Rodeo Drive in Beverly Hills. I have come to know and love him like few men I have ever known. In the library of people I respect, admire, and love, Bruce is way up there on the top shelf.

HUNTER ENIS and DICK LOWE

Late in life these two men have become part of the inner circle of my close confidants. When the apostle Paul talked about his "fellow workers" in the New Testament, he used a word from which we derive our word *synergy*. Hunter and Dick are synergy personified.

Hunter was my childhood athletic hero. We came from the same neighborhood, and when I was a boy, I watched him play high school football, college football at TCU, and then professional football in the NFL. After his playing days, he was a professional coach. While serving as offensive coordinator of the New York Giants, he was enticed to return to Texas and enter the oil business. After teaming up with Dick, they hit it big—or should I say *huge*—in what is known as the Barnett Shale. Hunter is the kind of guy who never forgets his roots. Our old high school principal at Poly High always signed off the intercom with these words: "Always remember who you are and where you are from!" And Hunter always has and always does. The true test of people of influence and character is their kindness to someone who can be of little help to them. This is Hunter and Shirley Enis. They do more for more people in the normal traffic patterns of life than any couple I know.

Then there is Dick Lowe, and there are few men I have ever known whom I love more than Dick. He and his wife, Mary, have left their footprints all over their city, through homeless shelters and cancer centers and a thousand other venues in between. Countless individuals have been caught up in their incredible flow.

Of course, those who know Dick know his name is synonymous with TCU football. He lives it; he breathes it. It is through Dick and Hunter that I have become a close friend and confidant of Gary Patterson, whom we all consider to be the greatest coach and influencer with vision, integrity, and purpose to be found anywhere. Dick and Hunter also have brought into our lives some of our favorite people, like Jerre and Melba Todd and Dan and June Jenkins. As Dan wrote in his most recent book, he is counting on me to get him to "the peaceful shore." I am convincing him that only Jesus can accomplish that task!

SUSIE HAWKINS

Hands down. No one else is even a close second. The matter is not up for discussion. She is the single most influential person in my life—and has been since the first day I laid eyes on her. As I type these words, I only wish my vocabulary could really do her justice. Her outer beauty is eclipsed only by her inner beauty: she is the most selfless and sacrificial person I have ever known. She is also the superglue that holds our family together.

We share our love in the three different ways that the Greeks referred to love. One speaks of a godly love that is imparted to us from Him. This love always seeks the other's highest good. Another is a fondness, an affection, a "liking" kind of love that produces true friendship. The last one is a passionate, physical kind of love between a man and a woman—that spark that exists in the physical dimension. Our marriage is blessed with all three. We share this latter kind of love for sure. We still burn candles in our home that are not for religious purposes! We also have a solid friendship. She is my dearest friend, and I really like everything about her. But most important, we share that God-love that truly makes us one. She is the most Christlike human being I have ever known, and each passing day makes me want to be more like her.

Susie was blessed with a wonderful mom and dad, Don

and Nelle Cavness. Don was another of my most unforgettable influencers. A true leader in every sense of the word, he gave Susie what money could never buy: a secure and meaningful relationship between father and daughter. He died over twenty years ago and, since then, his longtime best friend, Doyle Hickerson, has been a welcome addition to our family as Nelle's husband.

Finally, Wendy and Holly, the products of our love, and their husbands, Brian and David, are everything any parent could ever desire in their children. I only wish I influenced their lives as much as they do mine. And now for the best part: these four wonderful people have given us Jackson, Halle, Julia, Hayes, Audrey, and Truett. Life is good, and we are so grateful.

Mission:Dignity

All of the author's royalties and any proceeds from *The VIP* go to the support of Mission:Dignity, a ministry of Dallas-based GuideStone Financial Resources that enables thousands of retired ministers (and, in most cases, their widows) who are living near the poverty level to live out their days with dignity and security. Many of them spent their pastoral ministries in small churches that were unable to provide adequately for their retirement. They also lived in church-owned parsonages and, upon their vocational retirement, had to vacate them as well. Mission:Dignity is a way of letting these good and godly servants know they are not forgotten and will be cared for in their declining years.

All of the expenses of this ministry are paid out of an endowment that has been raised for such, so that everyone who gives to Mission:Dignity can be assured that every cent of their gift goes to one of these precious saints in need.

For additional information regarding this ministry, please go to www.guidestone.org and click on the Mission:Dignity icon, or call toll-free 1-888-98-GUIDE (1-888-984-8433).

About the Author

For more than twenty-five years, O. S. Hawkins served pastorates including the First Baptist Church in Fort Lauderdale, Florida, and the First Baptist Church in Dallas, Texas. A native of Fort Worth, he has three earned degrees (BBA, MDiv, and DMin) as well as several honorary degrees. He is president of GuideStone Financial Resources, which serves over 250,000 pastors, church staff members, missionaries, doctors, nurses, university professors, and other workers in various Christian organizations with their retirement and benefit service needs. He is the author of more than twenty-five books, including the bestselling devotionals *The Joshua Code*, *The Jesus Code*, and *The James Code*. He preaches regularly at conferences, universities, business groups, and churches across the nation. He and his wife, Susie, have two married daughters and six grandchildren.

Follow O. S. Hawkins on Twitter @oshawkins

Visit www.oshawkins.com for hundreds of free leadership and personal growth resources.